DSM-III-R
TRAINING GUIDE
FOR DIAGNOSIS OF
CHILDHOOD DISORDERS

DSM-III-R
TRAINING GUIDE
FOR DIAGNOSIS OF
CHILDHOOD DISORDERS

by
JUDITH L. RAPOPORT, M.D.
and
DEBORAH R. ISMOND, M.A.

BRUNNER/MAZEL, *Publishers* • New York

Library of Congress Cataloging-in-Publication Data

Rapoport, Judith L.
    DSM-III-R training guide for diagnosis of childhood disorders / by
Judith L. Rapoport and Deborah R. Ismond.
        p. cm.
    Rev. ed. of: DSM-III training guide for diagnosis of childhood
disorders, 1984.
    Bibliography: p.
    Includes index.
    ISBN 0–87630–509–5. — ISBN 0–87630–563–X (pbk.)
    1. Mental illness—Diagnosis.   2. Child psychopathology—
Classification.   3. Diagnostic and statistical manual of mental
disorders.   I. Ismond, Deborah R.   II. Rapoport, Judith
L. DSM-III training guide for diagnosis of childhood
disorders.   III. Title.
    [DNLM: 1. Mental Disorders—classification   2. Mental Disorders—
diagnosis.   3. Mental Disorders—in infancy & childhood.   WS 350
R219d]
RJ503.5.R36   1989
618.92'89075–dc20
DNLM/DLC
for Library of Congress   89–10005
                                                                                  CIP

Tables listing DSM-III-R diagnostic criteria and DSM-III-R classification and related material are
reprinted with permission from the Diagnostic and Statistical Manual of Mental Disorders
(Third Edition Revised). Copyright 1987 American Psychiatric Association.

Copyright © 1990 by Judith L. Rapoport and Deborah R. Ismond

Published by
BRUNNER/MAZEL, INC.
19 Union Square
New York, New York 10003

MANUFACTURED IN THE UNITED STATES OF AMERICA
10   9   8   7   6   5   4   3   2

Contents

Tables

Preface

In 1987, when the American Psychiatric Association published its revised third edition of the *Diagnostic and Statistical Manual* (DSM-III-R), it was clear that we needed to revise the *DSM-III Training Guide for Diagnosis of Childhood Disorders* in order to reflect the changes as they pertain to pediatric diagnosis. As the introduction to the APA revision notes, the DSM-III contained cases in which certain criteria were unclear, inconsistent, or contradictory; and evidence from new research indicated that findings were inconsistent with some DSM-III criteria. The forthcoming publication of ICD-10 was an added incentive for updating the classification structure to rectify confusing issues and to reclassify disorders that were out of line with scientific and clinical evidence. In addition, the reclassification process was used to make minor numbering changes to ensure compatibility with ICD codes.

Although there were mixed feelings about the timing of DSM-III-R's release, the implementation of DSM-III-R is desirable not only to promote accurate decisions concerning diagnosis, treatment, and management of patients with psychiatric disorders, but also to foster dialogue within the profession and continued research efforts. It is hoped that DSM-III-R, like its predecessors, will help to create a diagnostic consensus among practitioners and encourage a more reliable and valid diagnostic practice.

The need to revise this guide on childhood disorders was further intensified by our belief that diagnostic uniformity is essential for research on and clinical treatment of children and adolescents; therefore, taken together, DSM-III-R and this *Training Guide* will help to create and encourage such a consensus. Increased interest in and attention to diagnosis and classification of childhood psychopathology since 1984 has made the revision of this guide a substantial but nevertheless gratifying task.

Indication of this new interest is seen in the advent of several recent scholarly works in the field. Of particular note is the impressive volume *Assessment and Diagnosis in Child Psychopathology* (Rutter et al., 1988), in which general methodological issues and the relationship between DSM-III and ICD-9 are particularly well covered.

Another major publication on diagnosis and measurement of disturbed behavior in children and adolescents is the special issue of the *Psychopharmacology Bulletin* (Rapoport & Conners, 1985). Although the issue is primarily focused on the use of measurement and assessment tools within pediatric psychopharmacology, sections are also included on structured diagnostic interviews, evaluation of social skills, as well as specialized scales for disorders not previously studied in depth such as Obsessive Compulsive Disorder, other anxiety disorders, and eating disorders. Such instruments provide the data from which diagnoses are derived and are an essential link in furthering communication across clinical and research centers.

Introduction

The study of any type of phenomenon requires a system for grouping and labeling events. In the mental health field, the *Diagnostic and Statistical Manual* (DSM) is such a formulation. It intends to provide an organizational structure for categorizing descriptive clinical information, whether introspective, biological, or social. In order to fulfill its function, such a formulation needs to be broad enough in its descriptive capacity to include all observations of pathology. Therefore, by nature, it will tend to encourage an ongoing process of definition and refinement. In the case of the DSM, this process is actively emerging as a dynamic function of increased knowledge and expanded application of the terminology and concepts of psychiatric disorders within both clinical and research settings. As inputs from new observations and broad-based applications throw light on the reliability and validity of its observed categories, the process of revision and refinement will continue. Medical science has successfully employed a similar approach, and we hope that psychiatry will be equally rewarded in its endeavor to identify causes, predict outcomes, and establish effective treatments.

Opponents of this descriptive categorization argue that the diagnostic process may lead to erroneous conclusions about underlying biological or psychological handicaps. There is apprehension that the stigma of a psychiatric label leads to a self-fulfilling prophecy; such concern is expressed with particular vehemence when children are concerned. Evidence does exist indicating that a child's potential and ability are influenced by expectations and attitudes. However, the designation of a diagnostic term does not parallel the use of labels by the public to identify the deviant. A psychiatric explanation may, in some instances, ease social expectations and foster patience and encouragement in place of punishment and derision.

The diagnostic categories delineated in DSM-III-R attempt to systematically and comprehensively describe psychopathology as it is encountered in clinical practice. For the most part, it has successfully avoided making assumptions about underlying etiology and has focused on description of behavior. In many cases it has expanded its descriptive capability by including symptom lists and threshold guidelines within the diagnostic criteria. Such attempts at clarification and descriptive consistency can only help in the process of analyzing diagnostic validity and reliability.

Diagnosis serves several purposes, as outlined clearly by Spitzer and Cantwell (1980). It first addresses the question "Is there a disorder present and, if so, does it fit a known syndrome?" In addition to classification issues, diagnosis is important for identifying the influences on and possible causes of the disorder in terms of family conflict, biological endowment, and social roots. A complete case formulation also addresses the forces promoting normal development. A thorough evaluation is the key to answering diagnostic questions and to planning successful treatment.

This handbook offers further clarification and definition of the terms and concepts included in the DSM-III-R criteria for disorders pertaining specifically to children and adolescents. Although DSM-III-R devotes a section to psychopathology arising during these early years, other psychiatric disorders, such as Anxiety, Obsessive Compulsive Disorder, Depression, and Schizophrenia, also occur in childhood and adolescence. The diagnostic criteria for these are largely the same for children and adults, but particular issues emerge when making differential diagnoses of these disorders in children. It is our hope that use of this guide will help to create a diagnostic consensus among practitioners and encourage a diagnostic practice leading to greater reliability and validity.

Within this guide, commentary is given on the manifestation of disorders, differentiation among syndromes, and quality of characteristics, along with descriptive case material illustrating clinical symptoms. Troublesome areas are indicated, with the hope that increased clinical awareness and record keeping will lead to more accurate classification in the future. The multiaxial approach of DSM is highlighted as a means of assessing the child from a variety of perspectives. It focuses on the exogenous factors influencing development, sources of disorder, as well as the child's limitations and capabilities.

As a phenomenological model, the DSM structure will require major changes and minor adjustments. The user must strive for an objective

attitude toward diagnosis, realizing the benefits of conscientiously applying diagnostic guidelines without slavish adherence to every detail. In
many instances, seemingly clear, precise descriptions of behavior call for
judgments that are difficult and subjective. The diagnostic system is a
valuable tool when used with care and with a mind toward further
improvement. It may be that DSM-IV will stipulate laboratory measures
as validation of, or even as criteria for, certain diagnoses. If that were to
happen, there would be drastic revisions in the grouping of disorders.
Enlightened application of the principles of DSM-III-R will certainly
influence the future of psychiatric diagnosis.

An Overview of Psychiatric Diagnosis in Pediatric Age Groups

Chapter 1

Historical Perspective on Diagnosis of Childhood Disorders

Child psychiatry is a very recent addition to the scientific study and treatment of mental disorders. Around the turn of the century, Binet introduced the first psychometric measure for children, but the scale was not used in this country until after 1910. This occurrence was closely followed by the application of psychoanalytic theory, which strongly influenced child psychiatry in that it viewed childhood experience as a determinant of adult psychopathology. The emphasis placed on the meaning of childhood events and their influence on later psychiatric disturbance evoked interest in obtaining information directly from children.

Dr. Leo Kanner's textbook *Child Psychiatry* (Kanner, 1935) was a milestone for American child psychiatry, marking its birth as a specialty in this country. Dr. Kanner's expositions served as a model of descriptive clarity and increased awareness and interest in the types of children depicted. His description of infantile autism is a well-known example. Dr. Kanner's text still provides one of the clearest examples for diagnosis in child psychiatry; in fact, in several instances, the DSM categories have little to add.

During the past 50 years, there has been an explosion of information describing human behavior at all ages, documenting developmental changes and explaining mechanisms and processes of change. Although child

3

psychologists have formulated assessment techniques and have designed tests in a variety of cognitive and behavioral areas, the impact on research techniques has remained minimal except in the area of psychometric testing.

Perhaps the two most important influences on modern diagnosis and measurement in child psychiatry have been the areas of psychopharmacology in this country and psychiatric epidemiology in Great Britain. The contribution of the Isle of Wight study (Rutter et al., 1970) cannot be overstated. Among other findings are the relative frequency of behavioral disturbance in childhood, the powerful nonspecific association between neurological impairments and behavioral disorders, and the association of Specific Developmental Disorder with Conduct Disorder. These findings remain a major influence on current research in the field.

During the 1950s psychopharmacology brought about dramatic changes in both patient care and the direction of research and assessment in general psychiatry in the United States and in Europe. The advent of new medications created renewed interest in describing changes in symptomatology directly attributable to treatment efficacy. This resulted in the development of rating scales and the use of double-blind techniques and increased the amount of attention placed on diagnosis in the prediction of outcome.

Pediatric psychopharmacology took considerably longer to get started, despite early reports of the efficacy of stimulants for treatment of behavioral disorders in children (Bradley, 1937) and general interest in child development in the 1930s and 1940s. The use of rating scales to record initial symptom levels and subsequent changes has had a potent effect on present-day clinical descriptions and ratings. It is not surprising that major influential textbooks on pediatric psychopharmacology (Weiner, 1977; Werry, 1978) emphasized the importance of measurement and diagnosis. The goal of physiological dissection of syndromes on the basis of drug response (though not particularly realized in child psychiatry [Rapoport, 1985] but an excellent heuristic principle) has led to careful delineation of syndromes among children participating in drug-research trials.

Although in its early stages psychopharmacological research sparked acute interest in childhood diagnosis, an intrinsically practical question emerged: Would the same medication work for similar or different indications? Thus, distinctions noted between autism and Schizophrenia, or between Attention-Deficit Hyperactivity Disorder and Conduct Disorder, assisted in decisions concerning treatment and in the prediction of outcome.

It is no accident that almost half of the DSM committee on disorders of childhood and adolescence consisted of researchers who were working in pediatric psychopharmacology.

It is ironic that stimulant medications, which have a diagnostically nonspecific effect (Rapoport, 1985), comprise the only group of compounds that have influenced the most accurate clinical description in modern child psychiatry research. The very speed and reliability of the effects of such medications have inspired numerous junior clinicians and researchers to document the influence of these drugs in a simple, objective fashion.

Development of assessment tools was a natural adjunct directly related to this increase in clinical documentation. Much effort has gone into validating rating scales and exploring interview parameters that might predict or reflect stimulant drug effects. Recent research has shown that virtually all children will become less restless and more attentive when given a stimulant drug, and that clinical efficacy depends on the individual. The optimism engendered by such demonstrated changes has had a profound effect. Perhaps simple, practical measurements, of such parameters as motor activity, have helped renew interest and faith in descriptive measures. Work with antidepressants has produced equally valid and reliable measures of change in depression, even in young children (see Rapoport & Conners, 1985).

Diagnosis is vital for child psychiatry, and the development and progress of this subspecialty have made the timing of DSM-III and DSM-III-R propitious for general clinical as well as research use. The impact of DSM-III on child psychiatry has been remarkable. Although intended for use in the United States, it has aroused intense interest in other countries, and literally hundreds of articles in the United States and abroad have addressed the accuracy and meaningfulness of the DSM system in child psychiatry as well as its differences from ICD-9.

As part of the revision of DSM-III, the APA sponsored three field trials, two of which were for childhood-onset syndromes: Disruptive Behavior Disorders and Pervasive Developmental Disorders. Because of this more extensive work, these two groups have the most substantive changes in DSM-III-R.

But the most important impact is harder to objectify—that is, improved communication within the clinical community and across research centers. Over the past decade, and particularly since DSM-III was published, child psychiatrists have increasingly appreciated the need for reliability and validity within a diagnostic system.

To further research on diagnosis of childhood disorders, a number of national and international efforts have taken place in recent years. The National Institute of Mental Health has sponsored several workshops addressing classification issues for Disruptive Behavior Disorders and Pervasive Developmental Disorders, as well as an international workshop to focus on discrepancies between and problems within ICD-9 and DSM-III.

Although pediatric psychopharmacology and epidemiology still provide much of the impetus for improved diagnosis (Rapoport, 1987a; Rapoport & Conners, 1985; Kashani et al., 1985), an impressive number of studies on diagnosis per se have taken place outside of these particular areas of investigation (e.g., Prendergast et al., 1988). DSM-III-R is the next step in clarification and refinement.

Chapter 2

Definition of Disorder

Classification is essential for scientific progress in any discipline. This is difficult enough in general psychiatry, but in child psychiatry additional difficulties make the diagnostic process particularly challenging. To begin with, there is great lack of information about natural history, familial patterns, and developmental aspects of most of the childhood behavioral disorders. Because of this, most diagnostic categories have been generated on the basis of what clinicians agree they recognize from clinical descriptions as fitting what they see in their own practice. The particular group of children seen and the type of clinic to which they go may vary widely among clinicians and introduce a referral bias, which means that clinicians' knowledge of disorders is limited by their experience.

Furthermore, there is wide variation in the degree to which child clinicians have been trained to be descriptive. Inferential recounting of a patient's difficulties is based on the quality of interaction with the child and his/her family or his/her extrapolations from fantasy. In terms of descriptive methods, general psychiatry is much further advanced than child psychiatry in having available standardized interview techniques and widely used rating scales (such as the Hamilton Scale for Depression). Several such tools are now being generated for child psychiatry, but they are still in the early stages of development and their effectiveness will depend on clear, descriptive communication and the ability to use multiple informants (see Rapoport & Conners, 1985).

Ideological debates about "caseness" versus "continuum" arise whenever the question of diagnosis is raised. This volume is intended as a companion to DSM-III-R, and so the disorders are discussed as if they were discrete entities. As Eisenberg has eloquently argued (1986), disease definitions may, in part, be social constructs. More important within bio-medicine, however, is the process by which so-called discreet entities, such as anemia, are inevitably broken down into even smaller meaningful subgroups as medical research advances.

PROBLEMS IN ASSESSMENT

Informants

Very few children, particularly those under age 15, are likely to be self-referred. Presenting complaints usually come from parents, school, community, or professionals who may have seen the child in some special testing capacity. As a result, the clinician must, in addition to the child, simultaneously evaluate the sources of referral. Agreement among other sources, the interviewer, and interview data (particularly with young children) is often minimal (Stephens et al., 1980; Welner et al., 1987; Kashani et al., 1985).

In the past few years considerable attention has been paid to the problem of agreement among sources, even when the same diagnostic instrument is used. Not surprisingly, there are some disorders, such as depression, where the child's report may reveal more "positive" informa-tion than the parents', (Kashani et al., 1985), while other symptoms, particularly "externalizing" behaviors, are more accurately reported by the parent(s) (Welner et al., 1987).

The problem is not simply of agreement or disagreement. In many cases, subjective states simply are not seen or understood by the parent, while the child may be unaware of how inattentive he/she seems. Strate-gies for resolving disagreement have been proposed that take these issues into consideration (Reich & Earls, 1987).

In periods of social, family, and educational turmoil, the diagnosti-cian must be alert to the possibility of referral bias and of weakness in the child's support system. Carried to extremes, this point of view can under-mine the diagnostic system. The point, however, is that the clinician must regularly consider the possibility that an external limitation—for example, a particular school situation—is handicapping the child. Similarly, there are unhealthy family situations in which a child cannot be supported, and no specific diagnosis should be given the child. The focus of typical child guidance "cases" can also shift when a family support system changes, such as when a parent remarries or divorces, when a child is born, or when a family moves away from an important caretaker. These types of events can and do influence the adult patient, and it seems only reasonable to give special consideration to similar stressors with pediatric patients.

The complexity is further compounded by the fact that weak support systems typically occur together with deviant behavior in the child, not instead of it. The V Codes in DSM-III-R are for situations that are a focus of concern but are *not* attributable to mental disorder. Specific problems are addressed by choosing from a list of codes the one that best describes the situation. The V Codes are described in detail in a later section. When a mental disorder *is* found in the child, Axis IV can be used to identify and code the severity of social stresses contributing to the child's difficulties.

Poor Self-Report Skills

The child's ability to communicate with the examiner can be limited by his age, language development, and conceptual ability. This is a particular concern when assessing expression of mood in young children. It is also difficult to obtain reports of motor restlessness or bizarre behavior directly from the child.

There are almost no studies on interview validity in preschool years, and play interviews are more likely to be useful in this age group (e.g., Stephens et al., 1980). In a study on interview reliability of using the Diagnostic Interview Schedule for Children (DISC and DISC-P [see Rapoport & Conners, 1985]), Edelbrock et al. (1986) found that test-retest agreement for children six to nine years old was lower than for any other age group and suggested that reports of six- to nine-year-olds may be too unreliable to be taken at face value.

VALIDITY AND RELIABILITY OF DSM-III-R DIAGNOSES FOR CHILDHOOD DISORDERS

Validity of Axis I and II Diagnoses

Since the publication of DSM-III, research data have been accumulated on the validity of almost all the major disorders. Epidemiological work has provided continuing evidence that most childhood psychiatric disorders fall under two broad categories: either "behavioral" disorders or "emotional" disorders. It is encouraging that the major "broad band" subtypes are distinguishable, even though great controversy still exists over how to further subdivide or whether such refinements are appropriate.

DSM-III-R still contains a mix of "tried and true" diagnostic categories along with others that have yet to meet the test of time, and debate still continues for some major areas. Considerable agreement exists about the validity of autism as a disorder, although disagreement abounds over the extent of its boundaries. Similarly, general agreement that Conduct Disorder is a valid category also prevails. New work has addressed the validity of the diagnosis of depression in childhood. Others have investigated the distinction between degrees of mental retardation made on the basis of IQ and have shown evidence of other validating characteristics. (Specific categories and the changes instituted in the DSM revision are discussed in the chapters that follow.)

Individual categories have been changed in DSM-III-R to address some of the more controversial entities. The criteria for Pervasive Developmental Disorders are more specific and have been moved to Axis II. Mental Retardation is also placed on Axis II in order to encourage noting other Axis I diagnoses. More detailed descriptors are given for Attention-Deficit Hyperactivity Disorder, and Oppositional Defiant Disorder now describes a more severe condition. Because subtypes of Conduct Disorder and of Attention-Deficit Disorder in DSM-III had been criticized, fewer subtypes are defined in DSM-III-R. The following DSM-III entities have been dropped from DSM-III-R.

Axis I

313.22	Schizoid Disorder of Childhood or Adolescence
314.80	Attention Deficit Disorder, Residual
312.10	Conduct Disorder Undersocialized, Nonaggressive
312.23	Conduct Disorder Socialized, Aggressive
312.21	Conduct Disorder Socialized, Nonaggressive

Axis II

315.50	Specific Developmental Disorder, Mixed

There are still many problems to resolve. But it is a tribute to DSM-III that so much work was inspired in the pediatric area based on enthusiasm (or lack thereof) for its categories. Important work remains to be done in order to clarify differences between hyperactivity and Conduct Disorders and between Anxiety Disorders and depression (a dilemma well known in general adult psychiatry).

Eventually, there may be biological markers such as chromosomal abnormalities or brain imaging patterns that permit new ways of organizing our diagnostic system. Some would argue that identification of the fragile X chromosome suggests just such an approach as well as the startlingly specific response of Obsessive Compulsive Disorder to new pharmacological agents (Leonard et al., 1988). For the present, however, none of these possibilities can take the place of the classic indicators of validity: clearly defined clinical description, associated features, and follow-up status.

Reliability of Axis I and II Diagnoses
DSM-III-R, like its parent, DSM-III, has a great many operational definitions and diagnostic categories that may overwhelm the beginner. The specificity of the categories has led some to think that diagnosis might be difficult because too many patients will elude classification after all criteria are applied.

Concern in other cases has been that if categories are too broad the patient will meet criteria but the diagnosis will not be clinically appropriate. A study using DSM-III criteria suggested that problems did indeed focus on Axis I disorders, but that the major problem was differentiating between diagnoses, rather than struggling with detailed criteria, as anticipated. DSM-III and DSM-III-R were not designed to provide a diagnosis for every child; however, in the study mentioned previously (Cantwell et al., 1979a,b), surprisingly few of the 24 cases were considered undiagnosable using DSM-III, and raters preferred DSM-III to DSM-II for each diagnosis.

A more recent study using DSM-III with both research and clinician raters similarly found that detailed criteria were rarely the problem, whereas differential diagnosis and the handling of mixed categories were the source of most problems (Prendergast et al., 1988).

Difficulties still remain, however, that will have an impact on further refinements. As Cantwell et al. (1979a,b) found, certain cases and categories presented difficulty because of their ambiguity. Also, some obstacles to diagnostic reliability on Axis I and II have been identified. For example, adolescent emancipation problems, commonly seen by practitioners, have no satisfactory V coding. Operational criteria for Adjustment Disorder were not sufficiently well defined in the previous version and are greatly improved in DSM-III-R. Newer categories such as Separation Anxiety Disorder (and for that matter most of the Anxiety Disorder categories found in the childhood disorders section) are still unfamiliar and probably not sufficiently used.

Multiaxial features are no longer novel. Practitioners familiar with DSM-III will not be so uncomfortable about leaving Axis I blank, although some may feel constrained to make a diagnosis when none is expected. With the shift of Mental Retardation and Pervasive Developmental Disorders to Axis II, it is anticipated that even more frequently Axis I will be blank, or possibly that a V Code will be used, while the primary or presenting problem will be coded on Axis II.

Interrater Reliability
If two clinicians cannot agree that a particular set of symptoms is present, then the disorder will not be studied well enough to define its course, response to treatment, background features, and other factors, in order to decide whether or not it is a valid syndrome. Although there are undoubtedly Axis I diagnoses of unproven validity, reliability of all Axis I categories has been shown. The presence of disorders as descriptive entities on Axis I and II indicates, at the very least, that clinicians in some numbers and with some authority felt that the clinical picture presented by each disorder appeared in sufficient numbers of patients and represented a diagnostic entity in the form described. Furthermore, it is assumed that communication about the described entity will occur with sufficient clarity since reliability was tested using interrater agreement in response to stating the descriptors. This certainly seems to be the case for broad categories. For example, users of DSM-III-R are likely to agree that a disorder is in the broad band of conduct versus attention deficit rather than depression versus anxiety. Disagreement within the broad categories is much more common (Rutter et al., 1979; Prendergast et al., 1988). Some critics think that both DSM-III and DSM-III-R make finer distinctions than can be reliably sustained, particularly within Anxiety and Depressive Disorders. At least in the area of childhood disorders, DSM-III-R has partially complied by eliminating several subcategories.

A formal study of interrater reliability of DSM-III, with particular focus on the disruptive behavior disorders, reveals adequate reliability following some preliminary training in the use of DSM-III (Prendergast et al., 1988). As yet, no study has been undertaken for DSM-III-R. But as the Prendergast study showed, diagnostic scheme is only part of the answer to good interrater reliability. A number of other diagnostic issues in child psychiatry remain problematic.

Chapter 3

Specific Diagnostic Issues in Child Psychiatry

AGE-SPECIFIC MANIFESTATION OF DISORDER
Childhood disorders are uniquely characterized by developmental considerations that are central to many of the diagnostic entities. For example, enuresis would not be diagnosed as pathological at age five or six but would be at age 12. Similarly, characteristics of many two-year-olds, such as obstinacy or resistance to change, would be considered pathological symptoms if they still persisted at age five or six, whereas in an earlier period they are considered part of a normal developmental stage. Numerous examples can be cited, and all raise difficult questions about where normal development stops and pathology begins. Separation anxiety is usual between eight months and two years of age, although this may not be universally true. It is not considered a pathological process, however, until ages three or four.

Diagnosis in Preschool Children
A central concern is whether or not any reliable and valid diagnosis can be made for preschool-aged children. A few follow-up studies support the predictive validity of diagnosis in young children (Wolff, 1961); however, psychiatrists are reluctant to utilize diagnoses at this age. Earls's work (1982) suggested that DSM-III diagnoses were appropriate even for three-year-olds, which would support the comprehensiveness of the system. Other data (Stephens et al., 1980) have shown that some be-

haviors such as hyperactivity or aggressiveness may be reliably assessed from diagnostic interviews in this age group. Other symptoms such as anxiety or depression require very different interview styles and assessment measures in order to determine diagnosis in preschool-aged children (Kovacs, 1986).

Adolescence as a Developmental Stage
The distinction between age and disorder is even more complex when considering the later developmental stages. Considerable debate has ensued over the degree to which adolescence constitutes a special stage requiring singular diagnostic attention. For example, a DSM-III-R category that was added to the DSM-III is Identity Disorder. Much has been written about identity problems in adolescence, and college health services often use this category. Although the strongest support for this subgroup has come from university health centers, these clinics do not have long-term contact with the patients they treat and cannot provide additional information concerning outcome.

The decision was made to retain Identity Disorder as a category in DSM-III-R, even though insufficient systematically described, long-term follow-up information was available. It may be that ultimately a substantial proportion of patients described by this disorder will be considered to have mood or schizophrenic disturbances, as has been the case for adolescent inpatients.

Follow-up studies of adult disorders tend to argue for continuity over time when studying a specific diagnostic group (Welner et al., 1979). Such studies must be pursued in order to know whether adolescent problems constitute a specific disorder such as Identity Disorder or predict adult pathology.

Like many diagnostic matters in child psychiatry, this area produces strong opinion but suffers from a scarcity of facts. The virtue of the DSM system is that it provides clear description and definition of disorders so that follow-up, family, and treatment studies can be carried out.

REACTIVE NATURE OF CHILDHOOD DISORDERS

The Question of Family Diagnosis
Another issue raised when making diagnostic decisions about children is family diagnosis. During the meetings of the DSM Task Force Committee

on Childhood Disorders, strong argument was made, particularly by family therapists, that psychiatric diagnosis must go past its focus on the individual patient. Family work has identified types of families and family processes that, if ignored, could lead to artificial labeling of the child as a patient. This argument is particularly compelling in instances where change has occurred in the family structure and behavior problems have originated at that time, as when a child becomes a victim of marital discord. There are a number of less obvious clinical situations in which the nature of the interactions within the family unit may seem the most salient aspect of the case. Family therapists point out that family diagnosis is, in their experience, the most useful treatment prescription and predictor of treatment response that can be made.

For DSM-III-R, the situation remains unchanged. A number of meaningful systems for family assessment and evaluation exist (e.g., Jacob & Tennenbaum, 1988); however, a reliable diagnostic format has yet to emerge. Until there is some consensus or validation of information about specific family diagnoses, the V Codes in DSM-III-R can be useful for child psychiatrists in dealing with this issue. For example, V61.20, Parent-Child Problem, or V61.80, Other Specified Family Circumstances, can be used to indicate that the primary target is the family. These are to be used either when the child has no diagnosed mental disorder *or* when the focus of treatment centers on family issues. Further goals for family therapists will be to identify reliable and valid family diagnostic entities, and to reach some consensus, so that these concepts can be incorporated into a diagnostic classification system.

Adjustment Disorder as a Diagnosis

A diagnosis of an "adjustment reaction" has been overused by child psychiatrists. Only one diagnostic entity of this nature is presently incorporated in the childhood and adolescent section of the DSM-III-R, that is, Reactive Attachment Disorder of Infancy or Early Childhood (313.89). This is a well-documented condition, perhaps the best validated of any of the infant diagnoses. It is anticipated, however, that in addition to using this specific disorder in the child and adolescent section, child psychiatrists will continue to make steady use of the series of Adjustment Disorders (309.xx codes).

The profession has been strongly criticized for negating diagnostic description by excessively using "adjustment reaction" as a diagnosis. Reasons for this practice may stem from a desire to protect the privacy of the child or to reflect an optimistic outlook for the child's future. The point is that diagnosis was rendered useless for communicating descriptive information. The DSM-III-R definition of the Adjustment Disorder series seeks to limit the use of "reactive" and requires that some description of behaviors be included. The time period of the reaction is limited to a six-month period, with the onset of the disturbance occurring within three months of exposure to an identifiable psychosocial stressor. In addition, Adjustment Disorder with Depressed Mood is differentiated from Adjustment Disorder with Disturbance of Conduct. This key feature permits follow-up to determine whether the diagnosis can indeed predict a different outcome or whether it is associated with the onset of another disorder such as Depression or Conduct Disorder.

One of the primary strengths of the DSM system, if used properly, is that it can provide the information necessary for its own revision. Any clinician who records such diagnoses and reexamines the cases at a later time, through follow-up, will be able to systematically check on the validity of some of his or her own diagnostic formulations. For example, do children diagnosed as having Adjustment Disorder with Disturbance of Conduct have a different outcome from children diagnosed as Conduct Disordered or those having Adjustment Disorder with Anxious Mood? Clinics and hospitals will be in a position to carry out this type of clinical study in an even more extensive fashion.

ROLE OF INTELLECTUAL FUNCTIONING IN MENTAL DISORDERS

The importance of intellectual functioning in school-aged children, as well as the indirect assessment of some mood and thought states, has led to wide use of psychological testing. It is used more extensively with children than in general psychiatry and is heavily relied on for diagnosis and treatment planning. Such evaluation is especially encouraged for children who have behavioral or academic difficulties in school, or for children with an early developmental lag.

A major change in the DSM-III-R was the placement of Mental Retardation on Axis II. This ensures the recording of accompanying Axis I syndromes. The high association of psychiatric disorder with Mental Retardation, as well as the differing emphasis placed on intellectual level by different clinicians, elicited a strong push to rate intellectual functioning on a separate axis in order to avoid the ambiguity that was present in DSM-III, where it was an Axis I assessment. In fact, the version of the International Classification of Diseases (ICD) used in Great Britain includes a separate level for intellectual functioning and requires that all patients be coded on that axis.

The problem with assessing intelligence as an Axis I function was that some clinicians chose it as the major diagnosis while others ignored it completely. DSM-III-R maintains other DSM-III improvements to this category. For example, Borderline Intellectual Functioning (IQ 71 to 84) is a V Code (V40.00) and is recorded on Axis II. Also, the mild, moderate, and severe distinctions in Mental Retardation roughly correspond to the IQ levels designated by the international system and its British version (see Table 1).

A potential problem with placement of Mental Retardation of Axis II, now that Pervasive Developmental Disorder is also an Axis II code, is that intellectual level might not be coded if Pervasive Developmental Disorder is present. This seems unlikely, however, since DSM-III-R urges multiple diagnosis in such cases.

DSM-III-R AND DSM-III:
MULTIPLE DIAGNOSES STILL IMPORTANT

DSM-III-R continues to use most of new diagnostic groupings introduced in DSM-III that either had no counterpart in DSM-II or were derived from the splitting of broad DSM-II categories. (See DSM-III and DSM-III-R comparison of childhood disorders in Table 2.) Multiple diagnoses are encouraged, except when a specific differential diagnosis is required, as is the case between Schizophrenia and Mood Disorders. A special consideration with respect to child diagnosis must be stressed at this point.

In light of the relative lack of validating information regarding diagnostic categories for children, why add to the confusion by using multiple diagnoses for the same child? An important potential benefit is that it will provide information on which to base later decisions concerning multiplicity of groups and in weeding out overlap that may already exist in such areas as Attention-Deficit Hyperactivity Disorder and Conduct Disorders. Oppositional Defiant Disorder presents another controversial illustration since it is often diagnosed together with Attention-Deficit Hyperactivity Disorder. Is there overlap among the two categories that needs further delineation? If, for example, the outcome of Oppositional Defiant Disorder, as it is now defined, is similar to that of mild forms of Conduct Disorder, the delineating structures will have to be scrutinized and modified in order to avoid duplication.

(Text continued on p. 23.)

TABLE 1
Coding of Intellectual Functioning for DSM-III-R and ICD/U.K.

DSM-III-R		ICD/U.K.	
Axis II. Mental Retardation		Axis III. Intellectual Level	
Subtypes	IQ Levels	Coding	IQ Levels
317.00 Mild	50–55 to 70	0. Normal Variation	
318.00 Moderate	35–40 to 50–55	1. Mild (Moron, feeble-minded)	50–70
318.10 Severe	20–25 to 35–40	2. Moderate (Imbecile)	35–49
318.20 Profound	Below 20–25	3. Severe (Imbecile NOS)	20–34
319.00 Unspecified	(IQ level is presumed to be below 70 but individual is untestable)	4. Profound (Idiocy)	Below 20
		5. Unspecified (Mental deficiency (Mental deficiency or subnormality NOS)	
V Code: (Record on Axis II)		6. Intellectual level unknown	(Not assessed)
V40.00 Borderline Intellectual Functioning	71–84	*Based on standardized test scores with mean=100 and a standard deviation=15.*	

18

TABLE 2
Comparison of DSM-III and DSM-III-R Childhood Categories

Axis I and II Categories and Codes for Disorders Usually First Evident in Infancy, Childhood, or Adolescence

DSM-III-R Axis I	DSM-III Axis
Disruptive Behavior Disorders	**Mental Retardation**
314.01 Attention-Deficit Hyperactivity Disorder	317.0(x) Mild
	318.0(x) Moderate
	318.1(x) Severe
Conduct Disorders	318.2(x) Profound
312.20 Group Type	319.0(x) Unspecified
312.00 Solitary Aggressive Type	
312.90 Undifferentiated Type	**Attention-Deficit Disorder**
	314.01 With Hyperactivity
313.81 Oppositional Defiant Disorder	314.00 Without Hyperactivity
	314.80 Residual Type
Anxiety Disorders of Childhood or Adolescence	**Conduct Disorder**
309.21 Separation Anxiety Disorder	312.00 Undersocialized, Aggressive
313.21 Avoidant Disorder of Childhood or Adolescence	312.10 Undersocialized, Nonaggresive
313.00 Overanxious Disorder	312.23 Socialized, Aggressive
	312.21 Socialized, Nonaggressive
Eating Disorders	312.90 Atypical
307.10 Anorexia Nervosa	
307.51 Bulimia Nervosa	**Anxiety Disorders of Childhood or Adolescence**
307.52 Pica	309.21 Separation Anxiety Disorder
307.53 Rumination Disorder of Infancy	313.21 Avoidant Disorder of Childhood or Adolescence
307.50 Eating Disorder NOS	313.00 Overanxious Disorder

(continued)

19

TABLE 2 (continued)

DSM-III-R Axis I	DSM-III Axis

DSM-III-R Axis I

Gender Identity Disorders
302.60 Gender Identity Disorder of Childhood
302.50 Transsexualism
 Specify sexual history: asexual, homosexual, heterosexual, unspecified
302.85* Gender Identity Disorder of Adolescence or Adulthood, Nontranssexual Type
 Specify sexual history: asexual, homosexual, heterosexual, unspecified
302.85* Gender Identity Disorder NOS

Tic Disorders
307.23 Tourette's Disorder
307.22 Chronic Motor or Vocal Tic Disorder
307.21 Transient Tic Disorder
 Specify: single episode or recurrent
307.20 Tic Disorder NOS

Elimination Disorders
307.70 Functional Encopresis
 Specify: primary or secondary type
307.60 Functional Enuresis
 Specify: primary or secondary type
 Specify: nocturnal only, diurnal only, nocturnal and diurnal

Speech Disorders Not Elsewhere Classified
307.00* Cluttering
307.00* Stuttering

DSM-III Axis

Eating Disorders
307.10 Anorexia Nervosa
307.51 Bulimia
307.52 Pica
307.53 Rumination Disorder of Infancy
307.50 Atypical Eating Disorder

Stereotyped Movement Disorders
307.21 Transient Tic Disorders
307.22 Chronic Motor Tic Disorder
307.23 Tourette's Disorder
307.20 Atypical Tic Disorder
307.30 Atypical Stereotyped Movement Disorder

Other Disorders with Physical Manifestations
307.00 Stuttering
307.60 Functional Enuresis
307.70 Functional Encopresis
307.46 Sleepwalking Disorder
307.46 Sleep Terror Disorder

Other Disorders of Infancy, Childhood, or Adolescence
313.89 Reactive Attachment Disorder of Infancy
313.22 Schizoid Disorder of Childhood or Adolescence
313.23 Elective Mutism
313.81 Oppositional Disorder
313.82 Identity Disorder

Other Disorders of Infancy, Childhood, or Adolescence
313.23 Elective Mutism
313.82 Identity Disorder
318.89 Reactive Attachment Disorder of Infancy or Early Childhood
307.30 Stereotypy/Habit Disorder
314.00 Undifferentiated Attention-Deficient Disorder

DSM-III-R Axis II
Developmental Disorders

Mental Retardation
317.00 Mild Mental Retardation
318.00 Moderate Mental Retardation
318.10 Severe Mental Retardation
318.20 Profound Mental Retardation
319.00 Unspecified Mental Retardation

Pervasive Development Disorders
299.00 Autistic Disorder
   Specify: if childhood onset
299.80 Pervasive Developmental Disorder NOS

Specific Developmental Disorders
Academic Skills Disorders
315.10 Developmental Arithmetic Disorder
315.80 Developmental Expressive Writing Disorder
315.00 Developmental Reading Disorder

Pervasive Developmental Disorders
299.0(x) Infantile Autism
299.9(x) Childhood Onset Pervasive Developmental Disorder
299.8(x) Atypical

DSM-III Axis II
Specific Developmental Disorders
315.00 Developmental Reading Disorder
315.10 Developmental Arithmetic Disorder
315.31 Developmental Language Disorder
315.39 Developmental Articulation Disorder
315.50 Mixed Specific Developmental Disorder
315.90 Atypical Specific Developmental Disorder

*These codes are used for more than DSM-III-R diagnosis or subtype in order to maintain compatibility with ICD-9-CM.

(continued)

TABLE 2 (continued)

DSM-III-R Axis II Developmental Disorders	DSM-III Axis II Specific Developmental Disorders
Language and Speech Disorders	
315.39 Developmental Articulation Disorder	
315.31* Developmental Expressive Language Disorder	
315.31* Developmental Receptive Language Disorder	
Motor Skills Disorders	
315.40 Developmental Coordination Disorder	
315.90* Specific Developmental Disorder NOS	
Other Developmental Disorders	
315.90* Developmental Disorder NOS	

*These codes are used for more than DSM-III-R diagnosis or subtype in order to maintain compatibility with ICD-9-CM.

The use of multiple axes is the primary force ensuring that multiple diagnoses and complementary characteristics are recorded. There is, however, considerable question as to the extent to which multiple Axis I diagnoses should play such a role. Implicit in the DSM system is the notion that multiple diagnoses will lead to better categorization. The ICD is in fundamental disagreement with this position (see Appendix I). Opponents of the DSM view think that multiple diagnoses beg the question and that crucial clinical decisions about salient features of a case would be (inadvertently) avoided. They also question whether or not overlap will be accurately and consistently recorded, especially since studies show that multiple diagnoses are not consistently applied across centers (Prendergast et al., 1988). Despite the differences of opinion, multiple categories are of express importance for the DSM because of the relative multiplicity of highly specific diagnoses.

Although the DSM urges multiple diagnoses and will continue to influence clinicians to make more individual diagnoses, critics are also concerned that important differential diagnoses will not be made because of such multiple recordings. This is not likely to be so. In the first place, mutually exclusive differential diagnoses are specified in the criteria for some Axis I disorders. For example, hyperactivity as a symptom may occur in both Attention-Deficit Hyperactivity Disorder and Schizophrenia. When specific symptoms can be accounted for by more than one disorder (such as Attention-Deficit Hyperactivity Disorder *or* Schizophrenia, to account for hyperactivity), the nature of the total symptom picture will determine the diagnosis.

In other areas, it will be evident that some diagnoses, at least descriptively, are mild forms of another. For example, one would not make the diagnosis of Conduct Disorder and Oppositional Defiant Disorder, or Identity Disorder and Borderline Personality Disorder.

Some diagnostic combinations will remain murky. In practice it will be difficult to diagnose both Moderate Mental Retardation and a Specific Developmental Disorder, although they are specifically suggested as common associates in the DSM-III-R manual. Similarly, in our opinion, when IQ is less than 50, it is often difficult to support an independent diagnosis of Pervasive Developmental Disorder.

The greatest diagnostic confusion is created when children show signs of more than one disorder—the mixture of anxiety/depression symptoms with Conduct Disorder or hyperactivity, for example—and this will give rise to diagnostic debate. Here, by urging multiple codings,

DSM-III-R departs from both DSM-II and ICD-9, which would choose the salient disorder or else specifically code "Mixed Disturbance of Emotions and Conduct" (312.3). Studies show, however, that a multiaxial system goes a long way toward eliminating some of the confusion created by frequently associated disorders (Russell et al., 1979; Rutter et al., 1975; Stephens et al., 1980; Prendergast et al., 1988).

Basic Concepts for Pediatric Psychiatric Diagnosis

Chapter 4

The Purpose of
Axis II

In addition to Axis I diagnoses for the pediatric age group, several other areas comprise and complement the diagnostic evaluation. These derive from the comprehensive nature of the multiaxial system of the DSM and from issues related to collection of clinical information and the resulting implications for treatment. These underlying notions form an important framework within the diagnostic process and, especially for child psychiatry, will influence the direction of future study and knowledge.

The evolution of the multiaxial system of the DSM-III and DSM-III-R has been a milestone in psychiatry's quest for descriptive clarity. An axial system of diagnosis has been in use for over 25 years within psychiatry, and child psychiatrists have been its strongest proponents (Rutter et al., 1975). Discrepancies in diagnosis have previously occurred because clinicians chose to concentrate on one aspect of a child's problem while ignoring the presence of others or judging them insignificant to the presenting problem.

The Axis II designation for adult diagnoses is used for Personality Disorders; however, a special use of Axis II has been designated when diagnosing children and adolescents. It was designed to ensure that Specific Developmental Disorders, such as reading and language disorders, are always recorded. When they are highlighted on a separate axis, their importance is not overlooked in future treatment planning and some conformity is provided within clinical practice for coding their presence.

In DSM-III-R, a significant addition was made to Axis II by moving both Mental Retardation and Pervasive Developmental Disorders from Axis I to Axis II.

MENTAL RETARDATION

Mental Retardation was placed on Axis II primarily to ensure coding of intellectual level. Many critics of DSM-III felt that intellectual functioning belonged on a separate axis entirely. Understandably, reluctance to add an additional axis resulted in this compromise, the rationale for placement being that intelligence is fundamentally a developmental process. In the international classification system as used in Great Britain, however, intellectual functioning is coded on a separate basis. Besides Axis II coding of Mental Retardation, the only other option for making any official notation of intellectual functioning is the V Code 40.00, Borderline Intellectual Functioning, which is also recorded on Axis II.

The Borderline Intellectual Functioning code may be important for treatment planning or diagnosis when IQ is in the 71–84 range. A common clinical example is the child, without Specific Developmental Disorder, who is identified as a "problem" in an academic environment. Evaluation reveals a relative intellectual impairment in a setting where range of achievement is slightly above average. This scenario is typical in many middle-class areas. The V Code may be useful and should be used in such a situation. There are a host of social and philosophical issues concerning the merits of this label that cannot be dealt with in this context.

PERVASIVE DEVELOPMENTAL DISORDERS

The transition of Pervasive Developmental Disorders from Axis I to Axis II was more for conceptual consistency in keeping with the reclassification of Mental Retardation under Developmental Disorders. It is unlikely, however, that this disabling condition would ever be overlooked.

All disorders considered to be developmental in nature are characterized by disturbances in the initial development of basic functions. In Specific Developmental Disorders, functions of speech and language, reading, and arithmetic are specifically and selectively deficient. For Pervasive Developmental Disorders, severe distortion of functioning is spread over many areas: social interaction, language, and range of activities and interests.

The two categories within this set of disorders are Autistic Disorder, 299.00 (formerly Infantile Autism), which specifies that the disorder is apparent in infancy or early childhood, and Pervasive Developmental Disorder Not Otherwise Specified (299.80).

For a more detailed discussion and critique of this change and the elimination of the subgroups as outlined in DSM-III-R based on age of onset, refer to Chapter 9.

The description of Autistic Disorder in DSM-III-R is much better than in DSM-III, even though there are no fundamental changes in the concept of the disorder. Behavior must be severely impaired for the person's developmental level in three spheres: social interaction, verbal and nonverbal communication, and imaginative activity. This category is of great research interest, and differences between the two subtypes must be carefully delineated, at least phenomenologically, in order to facilitate future study. There is, for example, speculation that Autistic Disorder is not so closely related to Schizophrenia (Green et al., 1984; Petty et al., 1984); however, until biological or other measures are derived that will validate separate categories, the descriptive approach of DSM-III-R seems the best available.

SPECIFIC DEVELOPMENTAL DISORDERS

The separate axis notation of Specific Developmental Disorders is made even when psychiatric disorder is absent on Axis I. Multiple coding permits examination of the frequency and type of Specific Developmental Disorders associated with Axis I disorders. There is already evidence of associations between Specific Developmental Disorders and some Axis I diagnoses—for example, the well-known affiliation between Conduct Disorder and Developmental Reading Disorder and at least nonspecific associations between speech and language delays and several Axis I disorders (Cantwell & Baker, 1985). The extent to which other specific disorders are connected to particular psychiatric syndromes is less clear. Although controversy has surrounded the decision to include some of the developmental disorders as diagnoses of mental disorder, it is recognized that impairment of function and resulting distress are usually features of severe developmental disorder. In many cases it seems likely that identification and treatment of these disorders will come from the educational rather than the mental health fields.

Two Specific Developmental Disorders are new to DSM-III-R— Developmental Coordination Disorder (315.40) and Developmental Expressive Writing Disorder (315.80). The latter is commonly associated with Disruptive Behavior Disorders. The former has a long history of clinical use and is also included in ICD-10 (see Appendix I). Again, multiple diagnosis for Axis I disorders is important, as well as thorough recording of Axis II Developmental Disorders and level of intellectual functioning. Such information about this child patient group will be crucial for understanding treatment response and clinical outcome.

Numerous diagnostic issues are unresolved with respect to the Specific Developmental Disorders. To date, there is lack of agreement on psychometric or educational standards by which to quantify "developmental lag," a term used to describe the marked delay in relation to normal development. In addition, the pattern of development may be deviant and not simply delayed. Most important, the impairment must significantly interfere with school or daily functioning in order for the diagnosis to be made. Undoubtedly, there will be further subdivisions of Specific Developmental Disorders, perhaps on biological grounds, but distinctions with sufficient sensitivity or specificity have not yet been found. In the meantime, Specific Developmental Disorders represent a reasonable approximation of clinical description of a valid category of disorders awaiting further clarification and research.

UNRESOLVED ISSUES

Enuresis and Encopresis as Developmental Disorders

In the early stages of DSM-III, Enuresis and Encopresis were considered candidates for Axis II, along with other Specific Developmental Disorders. One reason for deciding not to include them was that a certain percentage of children with these disorders suffer from *secondary*, rather than *primary*, Enuresis or Encopresis. These children achieve voluntary bladder and bowel control, but then regress after toilet training is completed. This meant that Secondary Enuresis, for example, would be placed on Axis I while Primary Enuresis would go to Axis II. Having the same disorder on both Axis I and II seemed impractical. On Axis I, the distinction between primary and secondary conditions should be stressed as a matter of diagnostic significance, particularly for Encopresis and to some extent Enuresis. Although the inclusion of Primary Enuresis or Encopresis as a "mental disorder" is objectionable, these disorders should be noted because of their frequent, although not invariable, association with behavioral disturbance. Nevertheless, regular occurrence as an isolated symptom and the tendency for higher frequency among males make Primary Enuresis much like other Specific Developmental Disabilities. There may be cases where Enuresis is the sole presenting complaint and, in the absence of associated behavioral disturbance, the placement of this diagnosis as a Specific Developmental Disorder would have seemed more appropriate.

Chapter 5

The Use of Axes III, IV, and V in Pediatric Diagnosis

AXIS III. PHYSICAL DISORDERS AND CONDITIONS

The coding of medical or physical conditions on Axis III is a major part of the diagnostic formulation but will not be discussed here. These conditions correspond to those specified in ICD-9-CM. It is important, however, for the clinician to be aware of the major insights that epidemiology has given child psychiatry in relation to Axis III disorders. For example, the Isle of Wight survey (Rutter et al., 1970) showed a powerful association between *all* neurological disorders and *all* behavioral syndromes, even though the association was completely nonspecific. If significant conditions exist, Axis III will be important for the understanding and management of a case.

Although the official diagnostic assessment is formulated on Axes I to III, Axes IV and V code supplemental information.

AXIS IV. SEVERITY OF PSYCHOSOCIAL STRESSORS

Axis IV, which deals with psychosocial stressors, should be particularly helpful to child psychiatrists, in addition to whatever information is collected in specific clinical and research settings, since clinicians who treat children have been keenly aware of the importance of environmental supports for normal development and the significance of stress in abnormal development. This axis encourages the identification of major stressors that may have contributed to either the development of a new disorder, recurrence of a prior disorder, or exacerbation of an existing disorder. It also addresses the importance of situational stress in many childhood disorders. Such an evaluation can determine, to some degree, any significant relationship between the. type, severity, improvement, or exacerbation of Axis I disorders and social stressors.

Severity of psychosocial stressors (Axis IV) is determined by assessing the quality, character, and quantity of events within the previous year. The severity rating is intended to measure the degree of stress in relation to average experience and not to indicate the patient's vulnerability. The only exception to identification of stressors within the year is when evaluating for Post-traumatic Stress Disorder. In some cases the stress may be related to anticipation of a future event. In all evaluations the clinician is asked to determine whether the stress is caused by predominantly acute events (duration less than six months) or by predominantly enduring circumstances (duration greater than six months). In addition to the rating, the clinician should also identify the relevant stressors.

DSM-III-R has a separate scale for rating stressors in children and adolescents, listing examples to illustrate the acute or enduring state of duration (see Table 3). The scale is modified slightly from DSM-III, with "minimal" dropped. In addition the code of zero (0) now is meant to indicate either inadequate information or no change in condition. A seven-point scale now used to indicate severity is as follows: 1=none, 2=mild, 3=moderate, 4=severe, 5=extreme, 6=catastrophic, and 0=inadequate information or no change in condition. The clinician is asked to rate the stressor and not the patient's reaction to it. This judgment involves distinguishing the number and type of significant stressors and considering their total effect. (In the British multiaxial version of ICD-10, presence or absence of stressors and specific stressors are coded on Axis V—see Appendix I for comparison.) Stressors suggested in DSM-III-R as etiologically significant are:

- Conjugal (marital and nonmarital)
- Parenting
- Other interpersonal
- Occupational
- Living circumstances
- Financial
- Legal

TABLE 3
Axis IV. Severity of Psychosocial Stressors Scale: Children and Adolescents

Code	Term	Examples of stressors:	
		Acute events	Predominately Enduring circumstances
1	None	No acute events that may be relevant to the disorder	No enduring circumstances that may be relevant to the disorder
2	Mild	Broke up with boyfriend or girlfriend; change of school	Overcrowded living quarters; family arguments
3	Moderate	Expelled from school; birth of sibling	Chronic disabling illness in parent; chronic parental discord
4	Severe	Divorce of parents; unwanted pregnancy; arrest	Harsh or rejecting parents; chronic life-threatening illness in parent; multiple foster home placements
5	Extreme	Sexual or physical abuse; death of a parent	Recurrent sexual or physical abuse
6	Catastrophic	Death of both parents	Chronic life-threatening illness
0	Inadequate information, or no change in condition		

- Developmental
- Physical illness or injury (also noted on Axis III)
- Other (e.g., natural disaster, persecution, rape, unwanted pregnancy, out-of-wedlock birth)

In addition, a group called "family factors" has been added to address distresses encountered in the childhood years: cold, hostile, intrusive, abusive, conflictual, or confusingly inconsistent relationship between parents or toward child; physical or mental illness in a family member; lack of parental guidance or excessively harsh or inconsistent parental control; insufficient, excessive, or confusing social or cognitive stimulation; anomalous family situation (e.g., complex or inconsistent parental custody or visitation arrangements); foster family; institutional rearing; loss of nuclear family members.

Summary of DSM-III-R Changes
A major change for Axis IV in DSM-III-R is that clinicians are asked to specify whether the stressor is acute (less than six months) or enduring. In theory, this is an excellent idea, but as practiced in DSM-III-R, the value may be limited. For example, parental divorce and death are listed as "acute" stressors, while predominantly enduring stressors are parental discord and harsh discipline. To many, this will seem an arbitrary and unsupported distinction. There is a great lack of research on stressors and their effects on or relationship to childhood mental disorders. Future revision of the axis is expected once differences among types of stressors are clarified and evidence for the selective effects of some stressors for specific disorders is indicated.

By listing each stressor in order of etiological significance, it is hoped that the appropriate use of this axis will eliminate the zeal for "adjustment reaction" by providing a place to note stressors without avoiding or distorting case description.

In formulating Axis IV of DSM-III-R, there were many ways psychosocial stressors could have been coded. The choice of "Severity of Psychosocial Stressors" as the content remains a purely arbitrary decision. It is not clear on what basis the present scale was chosen or whether it is relevant to children. Adequate interrater reliability has been reported for Axis IV of DSM-III (Russell et al., 1979); however, for research purposes, at least with children, there are probably more interesting aspects of psychosocial stressors to code. For instance, the nature of stress (loss, parenting, economic factors) and the factors mediating the stress could be addressed. The supports available to handle the stress, rather than severity of the stress, may be the most crucial variables. With respect to specific stressors (e.g., divorce), data exist showing that a child's age and sex are important variables in prediction of outcome (Wallerstein, 1983).

AXIS V. HIGHEST LEVEL OF ADAPTIVE FUNCTIONING

Axis V measures the individual's highest level of functioning at the time of the evaluation and within the previous year. In several adult studies, there is considerable prognostic value from this measure, particularly with Schizophrenia. This type of indicator has been less studied with children; even if positive results are indicated, difficulty may arise in that the highest level of functioning is defined within a one-year period and therefore may be confounded with the duration of the illness. The limitation of one year may mislead ratings for disorders continuing for more than one year.

It is also possible, however, that directing the clinician's attention to the strengths of the child may uncover information important for the therapy of the individual child and also serve as an index of the child's functioning over time. DSM-III-R provides a scale (see Table 4) for coding Axis V. The scale is a revision of two scales used for measuring mental health and illness in adults and children (Endicott et al., 1976; Shaffer et al., 1983). Information is derived from three areas: social relations, particularly with family and peers; achievement as a student based on performance; and use of leisure time, which includes hobbies, sports, learned skills, and recreational activities.

Research focusing on the issues surrounding the contents of Axis IV and V is needed. Careful use of these axes can help to clarify the troubling dispute concerning "reactive disorder" and "adjustment reaction." By coding behavior on Axis I and social factors on Axis IV, the predictive power of both can be compared by follow-up studies or observation of treatment response.

PROBLEMS OF MEASUREMENT IN PSYCHIATRIC EVALUATION

By now it must be obvious that diagnostic practices with children differ substantially from those used with adults. In most instances, the clinician is required to use numerous resources in order to obtain reliable information and make an accurate evaluation.

TABLE 4
Axis V. Global Assessment of Functioning Scale (GAF Scale)

Note: Use intermediate codes when appropriate, e.g., 45, 68, 72.

Code

90–81   Absent or minimal symptoms (e.g., mild anxiety before an exam), good functioning in all areas, interested and involved in a wide range of activities, socially effective, generally satisfied with life, no more than everyday problems or concerns (e.g., an occasional argument with family members).

80–71   If symptoms are present, they are transient and expectable reactions to psychosocial stressors (e.g., difficulty concentrating after family argument); no more than slight impairment in social, occupational, or school functioning (e.g., temporarily falling behind in school work).

70–61   Some mild symptoms (e.g., depressed mood and mild insomnia) OR some difficulty in social, occupational, or school functioning (e.g., occasional truancy, or theft within the household), but generally functioning pretty well, has some meaningful interpersonal relationships.

60–51   Moderate symptoms (e.g., flat affect and circumstantial speech, occasional panic attacks) OR moderate difficulty in social, occupational, or school functioning (e.g., few friends, conflicts with co-workers).

50–41   Serious symptoms (e.g., suicidal ideation, severe obsessional rituals, frequent shoplifting) OR any serious impairment in social, occupational, or school functioning (e.g., no friends, unable to keep a job).

The Importance of Multiple Informants

As mentioned previously, the fact that a child does not initiate his or her own treatment affects the diagnostic process considerably. Parents may be worried that their child seems upset or unhappy, or they may be distressed by the child's behavior. In either case the child may or may not be aware of the concern elicited in others and has little input in the procedures that bring him/her to the examiner.

The child psychiatrist must balance his/her assessment, weighing the sensitivity and perspective of the informants, most often the parents. Parents vary in their expectations, experience, and tolerance of children;

TABLE 4 *(continued)*

Code

40–31 Some impairment in reality testing or communication (e.g., speech is at times illogical, obscure, or irrelevant) OR major impairment in several areas, such as work or school, family relations, judgment, thinking, or mood (e.g., depressed man avoids friends, neglects family, and is unable to work; child frequently beats up younger children, is defiant at home, and is failing at school).

30–21 Behavior is considerably influenced by delusions or hallucinations OR serious impairment in communication or judgment (e.g., sometimes incoherent, acts grossly inappropriately, suicidal preoccupation) OR inability to function in almost all areas (e.g., stays in bed all day; no job, home, or friends).

20–11 Some danger of hurting self or others (e.g., suicide attempts without clear expectation of death, frequently violent, manic excitement) OR occasionally fails to maintain minimal personal hygiene (e.g., smears feces) OR gross impairment in communication (e.g., largely incoherent or mute).

10–1   Persistent danger of severely hurting self or others (e.g., recurrent violence) OR persistent inability to maintain minimal personal hygiene OR serious suicidal act with clear expectation of death.

Consider psychological, social, and occupational functioning on a hypothetical continuum of mental health–illness. Do not include impairment in functioning due to physical (or environmental) limitations.

they may also disagree between themselves about the child's difficulties. Other opinions and informants are extremely useful in constructing a comprehensive view of the child's situation. A teacher's perceptions are valuable for acquiring information concerning inattentive, hyperactive, or aggressive behavior. Additional reports from other relatives or even community members may be helpful in understanding the severity and/or in determining the situational nature of the disturbance.

Some studies have systematically addressed discrepancies between informants, most often between parent and child interviews, with respect to particular disorders. In general, positive data are weighed more heavily than negative information. For example, if a child offers information about depressed mood or suicidal thoughts, this carries more weight than the parent interview in which such data is lacking. On the other hand, antisocial behavior or disciplinary action at school may be more reliably conveyed by the parent (Welner et al., 1987).

Psychological Testing
Psychological testing is more beneficial in diagnosing children than adults because of the strong association between intellectual functioning and many areas of behavioral disturbance. For instance, Mental Retardation and Specific Development Disorders usually require psychometric testing before the diagnosis can be made. The tester serves as an additional observer and can employ techniques for indirect measure of mood and behavior, especially important for children with poor self-report skills. Projective tests, however, are not particularly important for settling diagnostic questions (Gittelman, 1980).

Neurological Examination
Neurological examination has a relatively small role in the process of diagnosing childhood disorders. Its primary use is to rule out neurological disorders; it does not add substantially to treatment planning. Various childhood disorders are, however, associated statistically with neurological correlates, such as motor clumsiness and overflow with Specific Developmental Disabilities and Disruptive Behavior Disorders. Attention-Deficit Hyperactivity Disordered children are often described as having soft neurological signs or a mildly abnormal EEG. A major exception, however, should be noted for Developmental Coordination Disorder (315.40), a new Axis II category (see Chapter 17). It is anticipated that standardized motor examinations will be more widely applied as part of both research and clinical use of this category (see Denckla, 1985).

Interview with the Child
The feasibility of semistructured interviews for children, their thoroughness, and successful identification of homogeneous populations in research efforts suggest that such a tool is a useful addition to the routine clinical child psychiatric evaluation. Play interviews are used to assess preoccupations, conflicts, symbolic meanings, and the psychodynamics of the family constellation. For preschool children, this may be the only way to gain information in a reliable way (Stephens et al., 1980).

The interview with the child is particularly important in the diagnosis of Anxiety and Depressive Disorders. In these areas the child, even the young child, is the best informant. Direct observation of behavior varies in significance when diagnosing other disorders, however. For example, a child with Attention-Deficit Hyperactivity Disorder, particularly an older child, may not manifest signs of inattentiveness and restlessness during the interview. Although play interviews may be essential in psychotherapy for establishing and maintaining a relationship, they should not be depended on to assess symptomatology, as they usually will not identify symptoms like hallucinations, suicidal thoughts, or frequent obsessions. The use of some type of semistructured interview is essential to making a psychiatric diagnosis in children or adolescents (see Appendix II).

Use of Rating Scales
Even though Axis IV and V are rating scales of a particular sort, nowhere in DSM-III-R is it specified that rating scales are to be used in the diagnostic process; however, it is desirable that every clinician become familiar with some of the common scales available for rating clinical severity and change (see Appendix II). These scales provide a powerful means of communication across centers and furnish an efficient and economical way of following treatment patterns and predicting outcome. They can afford a base from which any clinic can establish systematic research. There has often been a negative reaction to the use of rating scales in private practice. Some clinicians are reluctant to use ratings for fear that they will detract from the more subtle clinical evaluation and establishment of rapport. This is seldom the case. In fact, many clinicians report that they are more free to explore other areas knowing that the presence and severity of symptoms have been carefully documented.

The choice of rating form depends on the type of practice, the time available for completing it, and the informants used. Included in Appendix II is an extensive listing of rating scales for use with children and adolescents. Guidelines for the use and evaluation of these scales are readily available. The Conners Parent and Teacher Questionnaire scales and the Achenbach Child Behavior Rating Form scale have proven very useful in numerous settings. The Conners rating scales have been successfully employed in the evaluation of drug trials as a means of tracking changes. As an initial neurological screening examination, the PANESS, or its abbreviated version, is helpful. For additional information on available scales and their uses, see Rapoport and Conners (1985) and Goldman, Stein, and Guerry (1984).

Changes Over Time

DSM-III-R is clearer and more specific than any previous diagnostic nomenclature, although there are still some instances when one must go it alone. One improvement in DSM-III-R is that it allows for the fact that some disorders change over time. In particular situations, it is extremely difficult to make an initial diagnosis; in other cases, the quality of the basic symptomatology has changed.

A criticism of DSM-III was the lack of flexibility in applying operational criteria for disorders in older children or adolescents. DSM-III-R may provide more leeway in this regard. For example, the new criteria for Attention-Deficit Hyperactivity Disorder permit more reliance on inattention and less on motor restlessness, if appropriate, a more likely situation in children over age 12 (see Chapter 12). Similarly, the DSM-III-R criteria for Autistic Disorder now list behaviors typical of older or less impaired children or adolescents, not just the behaviors seen in infancy (see Chapter 9).

The manifestations of the Specific Developmental Disorders vary considerably with stages of development and degree of disability. It is not always possible to diagnose disorders of speech and language during the first three years of life, for this is the period when speech normally begins. Developmental Reading Disorder is not recognized until the first few years of school. Diagnosis should take these age levels into account; for example, if a child is clearly below age level on a reading readiness test, but still below an age when reading is expected, as frequently seen with kindergarten students, diagnosis should not be attempted at the time. At later ages, reading difficulties may still be apparent, though less pronounced. In fact, it is common for previously diagnosed adolescents and even adults to continue to show persistent signs of Developmental Reading Disorder. In such cases, the disorder should still be coded, indicating its mild form, since there is no "residual state" code for these categories. Clinically, the boundaries between the different Specific Developmental Disorders are often unclear. For instance, many children diagnosed as having speech and language disabilities gain normal speech but later have reading difficulties. The distinction between uneven and normal development and Specific Developmental Disorders is far from clear (Cantwell & Baker, 1985).

Specific criteria are not spelled out for each of the Specific Developmental Disorders, and it is up to the clinician to come up with his/her own formulation, even though there may be differences in definition of terms. For some, a significant delay in reading may be one year below grade level; for others, it may be two. The specification of standardized and individually administered tests is, of course, helpful and necessary, but the clinician is left with more decisions to make for this particular category than for the other child sections in DSM-III-R.

Chapter 6

Treatment Strategies in Relation to Diagnosis

PATIENT AS CASE VS. DIAGNOSIS AS DISORDER

The diagnostic process answers the questions "Is a psychiatric disorder present?" and "If so, does it fit a known clinical syndrome?" During this procedure a great amount of clinical information is generated that assists in understanding the individual case and planning treatment and management of the patient. When treating a child, it is crucial to gain knowledge of the familial, social, and biological roots of the problem, of the forces maintaining the problem and both facilitating and hampering the child's development, and of the child's individual strengths.

If intervention is necessary, then the specific diagnosis is only one piece of the information needed in order to develop an appropriate treatment plan. A recommendation is made depending on the attitude of the family and child, the practitioner's own expertise and judgment, and, perhaps most important, information concerning the natural outcome of the disorder without treatment.

THE MYTH OF "ONE DISORDER—ONE DRUG"

Management through medication is likely to be the most complex direction treatment planning can take, and the issues involved require careful scrutiny. Of primary importance when this type of program is considered is whether or not medication is the right route to take with a particular child. An assessment needs to be made of the child's sense of helplessness, the significance of medication to the family and/or school, and the severity of the condition—whether or not it improves spontaneously or deteriorates. These factors may influence the choice of a particular drug or argue against the use of any drug at all. In addition, information concerning drug response within specific diagnostic groups and evidence of familial influence on drug response may assist in the selection of medication. Although the latter areas are topics of research, the implications for individual application cannot be ignored. For example, an individual hyperactive child may respond selectively to dextroamphetamine or methylphenidate. Treatment must be based on empirical data obtained on an individual basis. Two different clinical groups have shown preliminary evidence that a pattern of disorder within the family may influence drug response in offspring. In one study adolescents with positive history of Tourette's Disorder within the family were more likely to respond to haloperidol (Nee et al., 1980). Similar reports suggested that a history of lithium response in a parent was associated with a beneficial response to lithium in children with a variety of behavioral and affective disturbances and problems with impulse control (Dyson & Barcai, 1970; McKnew et al., 1981).

A promising area for psychopharmacology is the treatment of Obsessive Compulsive Disorder with serotonin reuptake blockers, of which clomipramine is the best studied (Leonard, 1988). This is of considerable interest for child psychiatry because almost half of these patients have the onset of their disorder in childhood or adolescence. Furthermore, it now appears likely that a variety of other disorders currently classified as Impulse Control Disorders may be treated successfully with this same class of drugs. If proven to be the case, this has implications for the classification of these conditions in DSM-IV (Rapoport, 1987a,b).

PHARMACOTHERAPY AND CHILDHOOD DISORDERS

Since pediatric psychopharmacology is still in its early stages, the DSM system will enable a systematic assessment of patients as part of research and will provide the methodology to address questions concerning diagnosis and treatment. In the past, most work has primarily used a target approach, focusing on changes in individual symptoms, for example, stereotypy or classroom restlessness, in order to establish the efficacy of drug treatment. Little is known of the diagnostic specificity of drug effect, and no relationship between drug and diagnosis has yet been established

(Gittelman-Klein et al., 1978). The information that has been collected thus far should stimulate further investigation of the relationship between DSM-III diagnostic categories and the choice of somatic treatment (Rapoport, 1987a,b).

A disappointing finding has been the apparent lack of efficacy of antidepressants in prepubertal and adolescent depression. Why this should be is unknown, although the possible greater sensitivity of children to environmental effects has been postulated (Rapoport, 1987a).

Mental Retardation

Limited work in pharmacotherapy of retarded children has focused on target behaviors such as stereotypy, self-abuse, impulse control, and hyperactivity (Sprague & Baxley, 1978; Aman, 1982); no data have been collected concerning the influence of retardation per se on drug response. Although evidence suggests that mentally retarded and autistic children generally show a poor response to stimulant medication, there may be exceptions and alternate (often lower) dosage schedules that could be important in individual treatment plans (Aman, 1982). It is not known whether the degree of retardation influences the likelihood of drug response or the choice of drug. For example, antipsychotics may be more effective in treating hyperactivity in retarded individuals than in children with normal intelligence, but this has not been systematically studied. Even though Mental Retardation is frequently associated with Axis I disorders such as Attention-Deficit Hyperactivity Disorder and Stereotypy/Habit Disorder and Axis II Specific and Pervasive Developmental Disorders, it is the authors' opinion that such additional coding should not be given when IQ is below 50. (Note: DSM-III-R has *no* IQ cutoff for the diagnosis of Autistic Disorder.) At present there is no satisfactory subclassification system for noting the presence of associated behavioral symptoms with Mental Retardation.

Pervasive Developmental Disorders

Considerable confusion with regard to drug treatment of these conditions has arisen in part from changes in diagnostic terminology (severe conditions were previously labeled "childhood psychosis"). Drug treatment remains an empirical and largely unsatisfactory approach to these disorders (Campbell et al., 1977). Phenothiazines, although not specifically useful for the primary deficit of these disorders (Campbell et al., 1977), are somewhat effective in the treatment of common secondary symptoms such as hyperactivity and aggressivity. Thus, while pharmacotherapy may prove a useful adjunct to treatment of the Pervasive Developmental Disorders, drug choice must be based on a target symptom approach (Rapoport, 1987a).

Attention-Deficit Hyperactivity Disorder

A major innovation of DSM-III was the separation of attention and hyperactivity problems from those involving behavior and conduct. DSM-III-R further sharpens these distinctions. The benefits of stimulant drug treatment have been carefully documented in regard to restless, impulsive behavior. The prototype patient referred for stimulant drug treatment has a diagnosis of Attention-Deficit Hyperactivity Disorder. These distinctions among classifications have encouraged investigation of the benefit of stimulants for individuals with Conduct or Oppositional Defiant Disorder without Attention-Deficit Hyperactivity Disorder and leave one to speculate whether or not Attention-Deficit Hyperactivity, Oppositional Defiant, and Conduct Disorders represent a continuum of impulsivity rather than separate diagnostic entities. Preliminary findings indicate that stimulants may also benefit "pure" Conduct Disordered children, thus producing clinical but not diagnostic assistance (Gittelman & Abikoff, 1986).

Tic Disorders

DSM-III-R permits specification of several types of Tic Disorders. It is only for Tourette's Disorder that response to haloperidol has been firmly established (Shapiro et al., 1973). A question in need of further research is whether or not haloperidol treatment is effective only for this particular category of Tic Disorders. It may be that all chronic motor tics (without a verbal component) and other "atypical" tics also decrease with haloperidol.

GENERAL GUIDELINES FOR TREATMENT MODALITIES

Assessment and identification of a disorder are only two aspects of the diagnostic process. The formulation and continuing evaluation of a treatment plan are vital elements of this procedure. DSM-III-R, however, does not claim to be a cookbook of treatment recipes, and its less inferential framework in no way implies treatment preferences for specific disorders. Treatment issues are much more extensive than diagnostic ones; yet that very fact inspires continued striving for clarity of description within diagnosis and research of treatment response in relation to disorder.

It is generally agreed that once a diagnosis is determined, all treatment decisions should first involve assessing the present severity and the probable outcome if the condition is untreated. Once the decision in favor of treatment is reached, timing becomes important; for example, if a situation appears to be resolving spontaneously, that may not be the time to recommend a new intervention.

Diagnostic and treatment issues may be conceptually different for many family therapists who feel that an appropriate diagnosis should be applied to the family as a whole rather than to the identified patient. This type of therapy investigates why the child has become the identified patient and how the family can be changed in order to provide mutual support when dealing with current and future problems.

If behavioral therapy is considered, an analysis of problem behaviors is essential, and objective rating forms provide an excellent means for doing so. Observing the frequency of problem behaviors and the circumstances in which they occur leads to an understanding of how the negative behaviors were acquired, formulated, and maintained. Compliance with psychodynamically oriented treatments, as well as with behavior therapy, is heavily influenced by the motivation to receive treatment, the ability of the child and the family members to relate to the clinician, and the quality of the interaction among family members (O'Leary & Carr, 1982). The family's past experiences with psychiatric treatment and their attitude toward therapy will be major factors in determining the kind of treatment they will accept.

Focus on the Family
The importance of the family in the treatment of the child is self-evident, and family report is inextricably entwined in the diagnostic process. Many feel that family diagnostic interviewing is the most appropriate approach and should be the major tool of child practitioners. At this stage there is no validated diagnostic system that is generally accepted by family therapists. It is possible that the V Codes will be amplified in the future and then more formal categories of family pathology can be proposed. At present, V61.10, Marital Problem, or V61.20, Parent-Child Problem, can be used by therapists to indicate that the interaction between family members accounts for the presenting symptom, for example, sibling rivalry, a difficulty with another relative living in the household, and so forth. Until some other method is installed, the identification and recording of certain family attitudes remain a practical consideration. The

clinician should in some way register those instances when parents bring a child for evaluation and it becomes apparent that the couple is seeking help for themselves. In such a case marital counseling becomes the most appropriate treatment and may not involve the child at all.

In summary, evaluation and treatment planning go far beyond identification of a disorder, and the diagnostic process is much broader than recognizing DSM-III-R entities. It is hoped that future research will specify treatment response so that it can become a validating feature of some disorders, but at this time treatment response is one of the least helpful features in validating a disorder, even in the area of drug treatment. The DSM system in no way removes the burden of understanding the "case."

Major Classifications and Differential Diagnoses

Chapter 7

Classification of Childhood Disorders in DSM-III-R

The DSM-III-R classification system lists 30 Axis I disorders and 16 Axis II disorders under the diagnostic grouping of Disorders Usually First Evident in Infancy, Childhood, or Adolescence. Although these categories represent diagnoses most typical for this age group, consideration of almost all DSM-III-R diagnoses is appropriate at any stage of life. In fact, initial investigation suggests that child psychiatrists are underutilizing many general categories when making childhood assessments because primary application of these diagnoses has been with adults. Common examples of "adult" diagnoses that can expect regular use are Schizophrenia, for children having a childhood onset of a thought disorder; Mood Disorder, for the increasing number of children who are recognized as having Major Depressive Episodes, Single or Recurrent; and Substance Use Disorders, primarily for the adolescent population. At least two studies found that more than 20% of children and adolescents seen at academic child psychiatry clinics fit unmodified DSM-III criteria for Major Depressive Disorder (Puig-Antich, 1982; Carlson & Cantwell, 1982a).

The diagnostic conditions clustered under the infant, childhood, and adolescent heading are not only pertinent to these stages of development, but conversely, these disorders may persist into adulthood. DSM-III-R rarely defines age boundaries, but in several instances age is specified within the diagnostic criteria and may be a key in differential diagnosis between child and adult disorders (e.g., Conduct Disorder and Antisocial Personality Disorder).

TABLE 5
Other DSM-III-R Categories

1. Organic Mental Disorders
    May occur at any age.
    a. Delirium is especially common in children.
    b. Dementia can occur at any age due to specific etiological factors.

2. Psychoactive Substance Use Disorders

3. Schizophrenia*
    Onset usually during adolescence or early adulthood.
    Note: There is *no* separate coding for childhood onset schizophrenia.

4. Delusional (Paranoid) Disorders
    These generally arise in middle or late adult life.

5. Psychotic Disorders Not Elsewhere Classified
    a. Brief Reactive Psychosis—usually appears in adolescence or early adulthood.

6. Mood Disorders[†]
    a. Major depressive episode can occur at any age.
    b. Dysthymic disorder may begin in childhood or adolescence, but usually begins early in adult life.

7. Anxiety Disorders (or Anxiety and Phobic Neuroses)[‡]
    a. Agoraphobia without history of Panic Disorder—most frequent onset is in late teens or early twenties.
    b. Social Phobia often begins in late childhood or early adolescence.
    c. Simple Phobia—age at onset varies. Animal phobias nearly always begin in childhood.
    d. Panic Disorder often begins in late adolescence or early adult life.
    e. Obsessive Compulsive Disorder—up to 20% of cases have their onset in childhood; usually begins in adolescence or early adulthood.

8. Somatoform Disorders
    a. Hypochondriasis commonly appears in adolescence.

---

*See Chapter 10.
[†]See Chapter 11.
[‡]See Chapter 13.

TABLE 5 *(continued)*

9. Dissociative Disorders (or Hysterical Neuroses, Dissociative Type)
    a. Psychogenic Amnesia is most often observed in adolescent and young adult females.
    b. Multiple Personality Disorder—onset may be in early childhood but it is rarely diagnosed until adolescence.
    c. Depersonalization Disorder usually begins in adolescence.

10. Sexual Disorders

11. Sleep Disorders
    This has been removed from childhood-onset section. However, Sleep Terror and Sleepwalking Disorders are generally first noted in childhood and are primarily childhood disorders.

12. Factitious Disorders

13. Impulse Control Disorders Not Elsewhere Classified
    a. Pathological gambling usually begins in adolescence.
    b. Kleptomania—onset may be in childhood.
    c. Pyromania—onset usually in childhood.
    d. Trichotilomania—onset usually in childhood or adolescence.

14. Adjustment Disorder may begin at any age[§]

15. Psychological Factors Affecting Physical Condition

16. Personality Disorders *(Axis II)***
    Usually recognizable by adolescence or earlier and continue through most of adult life, but should not be coded unless stability of pattern can be assessed with certainty.
    Cluster A: Paranoid, Schizoid, Schizotypal (odd and eccentric)
    Cluster B: Antisocial, Borderline, Histrionic, Narcissistic (dramatic, emotional, erratic)
    Cluster C: Avoidant, Dependent, Obsessive Compulsive, Passive Aggressive (anxious or fearful)

17. V Codes for Conditions Not Attributable to a Mental Disorder That Are a Focus of Attention or Treatment***

[§]See section in Chapter 15 on Adjustment Disorder.
**See corresponding diagnostic categories for Disorders Usually First Evident in Infancy, Childhood, or Adolescence (Table 6).
***See Chapter 15 on V Codes.   *(continued)*

TABLE 5 *(continued)*

Axis I
a.   V62.30   Academic Problem
b.   V71.01   Adult Antisocial Behavior
c.   V71.02   Childhood or Adolescent Antisocial Behavior
d.   V65.20   Malingering
e.   V61.10   Marital Problem
f.   V15.81   Noncompliance with Medical Treatment
g.   V62.20   Occupational Problem
h.   V61.20   Parent-Child Problem
i.   V62.81   Other Interpersonal Problem
j.   V61.80   Other Specified Family Circumstances
k.   V62.89   Phase of Life Problem or Other Life Circumstance Problem
l.   V62.82   Uncomplicated Bereavement

Axis II
m.   V40.00   Borderline Intellectual Functioning

18.   Additional Codes
a.   300.90   Unspecified Mental Disorder (Nonpsychotic)
b.   V71.09   No Diagnosis or Condition on Axis I
c.   799.90   Diagnosis or Condition Deferred on Axis I
d.   V71.09   No Diagnosis on Axis II
e.   799.90   Diagnosis Deferred on Axis II

In the following chapters, major DSM-III-R classifications applicable to impaired functioning in the pediatric age group are covered with respect to diagnostic criteria and differential diagnosis. Despite emphasis on classification, one must keep in mind that observation and recognition, description and identification are important links in the diagnostic system. Classification organizes the observations by the descriptions; in DSM-III-R, specific diagnostic criteria and differential diagnosis are the organizing factors. In order to make a complete diagnosis, DSM-III-R provides additional information for each disorder concerning associated features, age of onset, course, impairment, complications, predisposing factors, prevalence, sex ratio, and familial pattern. The following comments on these disorders should help the clinician to use DSM-III-R for childhood diagnosis.

In addition to the shift of Mental Retardation and Pervasive Developmental Disorders and the addition of some categories to Axis II, the major classification change between DSM-III and DSM-III-R with respect to childhood disorders is the placement of Gender Identity Disorders under

Disorders Usually First Evident in Infancy, Childhood, or Adolescence. Although this does not represent any conceptual change, it serves to make DSM-III-R internally consistent. In fact, the majority of patients seeking treatment for these disorders are adults, even though their symptoms almost invariably were first manifested in childhood or adolescence.

The format used in this section basically sticks to the organization of DSM-III-R's section on Disorders Usually First Evident in Infancy, Childhood, or Adolescence. Where differential distinctions become cloudy, several disorders are discussed side by side. Also included are two general diagnostic categories, Schizophrenia and Mood Disorders, which present special problems for diagnosis within the pediatric population. Some diagnoses are straightforward enough in their application that discussion is limited to instances involving differential diagnosis.

Chapter 8

Diagnosis of Personality Disorders in Children

DSM-III-R makes an attempt to provide Axis I parallels for children and adolescents with Axis II adult personality disorders (see Table 6). If the symptoms diagnosed in childhood persist after age 18, then the diagnosis would change to the corresponding adult personality disorder. In some cases, this seems to be a logical progression; however, in the case of Oppositional Defiant Disorder, Conduct Disorder, and Identity Disorder some disagreement is bound to ensue.

Most personality disorders may be diagnosed in children or adolescents, although there is less certainty at these ages that the personality disorder will persist over time. Antisocial Personality Disorder, however, is not diagnosed under age 18. Differential criteria for diagnosing personality disorders in children and adolescents are outlined in Table 7. Two new categories of Personality Disorder were introduced in DSM-III-R: Self-defeating and Masochistic Personality. Because these have no clear implications for child psychiatry, they are not covered here. A recent study demonstrated that Obsessive Compulsive Personality Disorder may be reliably diagnosed in adolescence (Flament et al., 1988), but the long-term implications of this diagnosis are unknown.

Manifestations of most personality disorders are often recognizable by adolescence or earlier. However, such a diagnosis should be made only when the characteristic features are typical of the person's long-term

TABLE 6
Axis I Disorders Usually First Evident in Infancy, Childhood, or Adolescence and Associated Axis II Personality Disorders

Disorders of Childhood or Adolescence	Personality Disorders (Axis II)
(Axis I)	
Avoidant Disorder of Childhood or Adolescence	Avoidant Personality Disorder
Conduct Disorder	Antisocial Personality Disorder
Identity Disorder	Borderline Personality Disorder
(Axis II)	
Pervasive Developmental Disorder NOS	Schizotypal Personality Disorder

If features continue after age 18, change diagnosis to appropriate Axis II Personality Disorder, although Conduct Disorder may still be diagnosed in adults if they do not fully meet criteria for Antisocial Personality Disorder.

TABLE 7
Summary of Age Criteria and Differential Criteria for Diagnosis of Personality Disorders in Children

1. 301.00   Paranoid Personality Disorder

2. 301.20   Schizoid Personality Disorder
(Note: Schizoid Disorder of Childhood has been dropped. A separate diagnosis was not felt necessary, and some cases would fall under mild forms of Pervasive Developmental Disorder.)

3. 301.22   Schizotypal Personality Disorder
In children, disturbance in content of thought may be manifest by presence of bizarre fantasies or preoccupations. If under 18, does not meet criteria for a Pervasive Developmental Disorder. A diagnosis of Autistic Disorder would preempt this diagnosis; however, the personality disorder would preempt a diagnosis of Pervasive Developmental Disorder NOS.

4. 301.70   Antisocial Personality Disorder
By definition, this Personality Disorder is evident by age 15 and is associated with a diagnosis of Conduct Disorder. This diagnosis is not made in children and is reserved for adults over age 18 who show the full longitudinal pattern.

5. 301.83   Borderline Personality Disorder
Diagnosis of Identity Disorder is preempted by this diagnosis if all criteria are met, the disturbance is pervasive and persistent, and it is unlikely that the disorder is limited to a developmental stage.

TABLE 7 (continued)

6. 301.50   Histrionic Personality Disorder

7. 301.81   Narcissistic Personality Disorder

8. 301.82   Avoidant Personality Disorder
Avoidant Disorder of Childhood or Adolescence is preempted by this diagnosis if all criteria are met, the disturbance is pervasive and persistent, and it is not limited to a developmental stage.

9. 301.60   Dependent Personality Disorder
Separation Anxiety Disorder should be considered first. Chronic physical illness may predispose the development of this disorder in children or adolescents.

10. 301.40   Obsessive Compulsive Personality Disorder
Differential for Obsessive Compulsive Disorder may be difficult. No true obsessions or compulsions are reported in those with this condition; however, if both criteria are met, both diagnoses would be coded.

11. 301.84   Passive Aggressive Personality Disorder
Oppositional Defiant Disorder preempts this diagnosis if under 18; however, if patient is under 18 and does not meet criteria for Oppositional Defiant Disorder, this diagnosis may be given.

12. 301.90   Personality Disorder Not Otherwise Specified

functioning. DSM-III-R attempts to show corresponding diagnostic categories for childhood disorders. Other personality disorders may be applied to children or adolescents when the maladaptive personality traits appear to be stable, although again there are virtually no data about their persistence into adulthood.

Borderline Personality Disorder should be diagnosed in children and adolescents rather than the corresponding childhood category of Identity Disorder provided that the personality disorder criteria are met and the nature of the disturbance is pervasive, persistent, and not limited to a developmental stage. The same is true for Avoidant Disorder of Childhood or Adolescence; if criteria for the personality disorder are met, a diagnosis of Avoidant Personality Disorder would preempt the former diagnosis.

Chapter 9

Developmental Abnormalities in the First Years of Life

The considerable interest in the behavioral disturbances of infancy, together with new research in this area, has led to perhaps greater change in DSM-III-R in the categories considered in this chapter than in any other section of this guide. This chapter covers two broad areas: Mental Retardation and Pervasive Developmental Disorder, both now coded on Axis II, and Reactive Attachment Disorder of Infancy, which appropriately remains on Axis I.

As discussed earlier, a major structural change in DSM-III-R was the placement of Mental Retardation and Pervasive Developmental Disorders on Axis II. This placement has generated some controversy, even though extensive data show that Autistic Disorder involves distorted development from infancy onward and is also associated with some forms of Specific Developmental Disorder as well as with Mental Retardation (Folstein & Rutter, 1987; Wing & Gould, 1979).

Rutter has also expressed misgivings about having *both* Mental Retardation and Autistic Disorder on Axis II because of the danger that only one would be coded (Rutter, 1988). Such an omission would be particularly regrettable because intellectual level is a strong prognostic indicator in autism. Adequate planning for services clearly requires that both intellectual level and autistic disorders be recorded.

SUMMARY OF DSM-III-R CHANGES FOR PERVASIVE DEVELOPMENTAL DISORDER

The overall concept of Pervasive Developmental Disorders in DSM-III-R is very close to that of DSM-III, but it is much better described with more detailed and explicit criteria. DSM-III-R classification permits two possible Axis II diagnoses in this category: Autistic Disorder (299.00—specify if childhood onset) and Pervasive Developmental Disorder Not Otherwise Specified (299.80). The subtypes Pervasive Developmental Disorder, Childhood-Onset, and Pervasive Developmental Disorder/Atypical, have been dropped since there was little clinical evidence supporting differentiation among these subgroups. In fact, little research was published on that subject at all after the publication of DSM-III. At present, it is thought that Autistic Disorder represents a very severe form of Pervasive Developmental Disorder, but no diagnostic subclasses of Pervasive Developmental Disorder have emerged. Although such differentiations are desirable for research on the nature of pathology or issues of prognosis, they are not necessary for clinical management.

The Pervasive Developmental Disorder, Childhood-Onset grouping was eliminated because of the substantial difficulties in determining the exact age of onset in many cases. This was especially true in cases of older children where information about early infant behavior was gathered retrospectively and was subject to parental bias. The frequency with which this determination was made retrospectively meant that the category could not be objectively determined. Little systematic or compelling research existed to demonstrate that age of onset constituted a distinct subtype. In addition, clinical evidence failed to support the diagnostic validity of this subgroup. Elimination of this distinction, however, implicitly discourages further investigation of the validity of real differences based on age of onset within this group of disorders. In Autistic Disorder, as defined by DSM-III-R, diagnosis now relies less heavily on reports of early behavior, usually provided by the parent. The current criteria describe behaviors typical of the disorder across different ages and maintain that onset be during infancy or childhood. At present, the age issue is addressed by specifying that childhood-onset symptoms develop after 36 months. Using the DSM-III-R criteria, a large group of children are likely to be designated Pervasive Developmental Disorder Not Otherwise Specified, with few distinctions other than Profound Mental Retardation with some autistic features.

A further criticism of lumping Pervasive Developmental Disorder categories together is the failure to account for a subgroup called "disintegrative disorder," which is included in both ICD-9 and -10 but has never been used or acknowledged in the DSM structure. In "disintegrative disorder" the course of development is normal or near-normal for the first few years, after which there is a sudden deterioration (usually over several months) in social skills and speed accompanied by additionally severe emotional, behavioral, and interpersonal problems; this condition is also known as Heller's syndrome. Other ICD-10 subgroupings comparable to Pervasive Developmental Disorder are shown in Appendix I.

In addition to being moved to Axis II, Autistic Disorder in DSM-III-R now possesses a more complete description than the criteria previously used to describe Pervasive Developmental Disorder, Childhood-Onset and Infantile Autism. Although the combination gives a more detailed description, several important items have been dropped: age of onset by 30 months, exclusionary criteria for presence of delusions, hallucinations, and incoherence.

Cases that do not meet the criteria for Autistic Disorder, and where impairment of developmental skills is not attributable to Schizophrenia or Schizotypal or Schizoid Personality Disorders, are classified as Pervasive Developmental Disorder Not Otherwise Specified. Delusions, hallucinations, incoherence, and so forth as symptoms are no longer exclusionary indicators. The extreme difficulty in obtaining evidence of the presence or absence of these features, particularly in individuals with profound to moderate intellectual and/or language impairment, is cited as the reason for this change. It has nevertheless proved to be a controversial change because some symptomatic aspects in older autistic individuals are thought to resemble residual symptoms in Schizophrenia (for example, social isolation/withdrawal, peculiar behaviorisms, blunted/inappropriate affect). Childhood onset of Schizophrenia is generally considered a rare entity, and quite separate from Autistic Disorder. No research has appeared on this subject since the DSM-III version was published.

AXIS II: MENTAL RETARDATION
Mental Retardation affects approximately 1% of the population, according to most estimates. However, for many within this population, progressive attitudes have advanced their rights and given them the opportunity to lead productive lives according to their capabilities. Such advances in treatment have recognized the importance of providing adequate facilities, educational and training opportunities, and individualized case management. In many instances of Mild Mental Retardation (85% of the mentally

retarded population), adaptive functioning can attain a level that allows maintenance of competitive employment. This raises questions about the appropriateness of labeling the condition outside a measurement of deficit academic functioning. For more severe cases, levels of attainable skills have been shown to be markedly influenced by environment, management, and training opportunities. Therefore, the course of the disorder will be affected significantly in levels of functioning in both directions—improvement or deterioration—and this demonstrates the utility of Axis IV and V in assessment of these individuals.

The relocation of this category to Axis II, to reflect developmental abnormality, underlines as a measure the basic characteristic of the disorder of intellectual deficiencies. Many view this as a major diagnostic improvement, for it will affect the attitudes surrounding the treatment and care of the mentally retarded and, one hopes, lead to further appropriate mainstreaming on one hand or, on the other, encourage the provision of facilities geared to more humane and individualized treatment. This move is thus applauded, even though the host of accompanying social and philosophical issues will not be dealt with in this context.

Coding

Mental Retardation is always diagnosed and recorded as an Axis II disorder, if criteria are present, regardless of the presence of other disorders. In addition, it is important to code any existing Axis I mental disorders. Those most commonly associated with Mental Retardation include Tic Disorders, Attention-Deficit Hyperactivity Disorder, and, as noted, Pervasive Developmental Disorder. The question remains, however, whether such coding is meaningful when IQ is below 50. In cases where Borderline

TABLE 8
Mental Retardation: DSM-III-R Axis II Codes

317.00	Mild, IQ 50–55 to 70 (approx.)
318.00	Moderate, IQ 35–40 to 50–55
318.10	Severe, IQ 20–25 to 35–40
318.20	Profound, IQ below 20 or 25
319.00	Unspecified Mental Retardation (Used when the diagnosis is assumed, but conditions make it impossible to administer standardized intelligence tests. Should not be used, however, if IQ level is estimated to be above 70. See V Code for Borderline Intellectual Functioning.)

Intellectual Functioning is appropriate, this is noted as a V Code (V40.00) on Axis II.

On Axis II, the clinician should code any Specific Developmental Disorders (in cases of mild retardation) if continued development shows specific deficits, as well as the presence of Pervasive Developmental Disorder. In Mental Retardation, the quality of impairment is a generalized developmental delay that seems to follow normal stages but lags far behind and may be arrested at early levels. Impairments seen in Pervasive Developmental Disorder, by contrast, are abnormal for any stage of development. Presence of Specific Developmental Disorder accompanying Mental Retardation is noted when the specific deficit is out of proportion with the capabilities demonstrated in other developmental areas. Before coding multiple diagnoses, clinicians should check the essential features for those classes.

Any physical disorders and conditions are recorded on Axis III, including biological factors of etiological significance or neurological abnormalities.

Axis IV and V are more useful in the present form in determining levels of functioning and adaptive behaviors. They should also be used to devise treatment plans and counseling for general living skills and placement decisions.

Differential Diagnosis
If IQ scores fall within the range of 71–84 and there are deficits in adaptive functioning owing to intellectual impairment, consider using the V Code

TABLE 9
Mental Retardation: Diagnostic Criteria

A. Subaverage intellectual functioning as defined by an IQ of 70 or less
     Clinical judgment may permit flexibility in using the indicated cutoff points depending on the degree of impairment, adaptive functioning, and individual considerations. IQ scores have an error of measurement of approximately five points (i.e., 70 = 65 to 75).

B. Impaired adaptive functioning
     Below standards expected for age or cultural group in terms of social skills and responsibility, communication, daily living skills, personal independence, and self-sufficiency.

C. Onset before age 18

for Borderline Intellectual Functioning on Axis II. Differentiation between Borderline Intellectual Functioning and mild forms of Mental Retardation should be made with care using all available information on functioning and performance as well as intelligence test results. Mental Retardation can and should be diagnosed if Specific or Pervasive Developmental Disorders are present. In cases where IQ is below 50, however, such multiple diagnoses are meaningless in our opinion.

When considering the presence of an additional disorder, the examiner must first account for all the symptomatology that can be primarily attributed to Mental Retardation.

A differential diagnosis of Dementia is required if onset is after age 18, but if onset occurs before age 18 and previous intellectual functioning has been normal, both Dementia and Mental Retardation are coded.

AXIS II: PERVASIVE DEVELOPMENTAL DISORDERS

This class of disorders describes extreme developmental abnormalities with onset in the first five years and that are not normal for any stage of development. Pervasive Developmental Disorder represents a distortion in basic development that primarily affects verbal and nonverbal communication, social skills, and imaginative activity. Basic psychological functions such as attention, sensory perception, mood, intellectual functioning, and motor movement are affected at the same time and to a severe degree. There is an accompanying diagnosis of Mental Retardation in most Pervasive Developmental Disorder cases. The DSM system avoids classifying these disturbances in the same manner as adult psychosis because of marked differences in the qualitative nature of disorders with psychotic symptoms. The DSM-III-R diagnostic criteria for Autistic Disorders are shown in Table 11.

Since Pervasive Developmental Disorders are extremely incapacitating, persons with this diagnosis almost always require special educational facilities. Drug management with antipsychotics or by doses of stimulants

TABLE 10
Pervasive Development Disorders: DSM-III-R Axis II Codes

299.00	Autistic Disorder
299.80	Pervasive Developmental Disorder Not Otherwise Specified

has little effect on core features but helps to control secondary symptoms such as hyperactivity, excitability, moodiness, destructiveness, and sleeplessness. This type of treatment may allow continued home care by assisting parents in behavioral management. If no gains are apparent, however, continued administration seems of little clinical value. Behavior modification programs may offer a degree of behavioral control but require rigorous enforcement on the part of parents and are likely to be ineffective outside a therapeutic setting. Factors considered most impor-

---

TABLE 11
299.00 Autistic Disorder: Diagnostic Criteria

At least eight of 16 items from symptom list including two items from A, one from B, and one from C.

A. Impaired social interactions
    1. lack of awareness of existence or feelings of others
    2. no, or abnormal, seeking of comfort at times of distress
    3. no, or impaired, imitation
    4. no, or abnormal, social play
    5. grossly impaired ability to make peer friendships

B. Impairment in verbal/nonverbal communication and imaginative activity
    1. no mode of communication
    2. abnormal nonverbal communication to initiate or modulate social interaction
    3. absence of imaginative activity, lack of interest in stories about imaginary events
    4. abnormal speech production
    5. abnormal form or content of speech; pronoun reversal; idiosyncratic use of words/phrases; irrelevant remarks
    6. impaired ability to initiate/sustain conversation with others despite adequate speech

C. Restricted repertoire of activities/interests
    1. stereotyped body movements
    2. preoccupation with parts of objects
    3. distress over trivial environmental changes
    4. insistence on precise routines
    5. restricted range of interests or preoccupation with a specific interest

D. Onset during infancy or childhood (specify if onset occurs after 36 months)

---

tant for determining prognosis are IQ and development of social and language skills.

Diagnosis of a Pervasive Developmental Disorder reflects qualitative impairment in social interaction, verbal and nonverbal communication, as well as marked abnormalities in activities and interests. DSM-III-R makes these criteria more specific than did DSM-III. Although in most cases it is clear that development was abnormal in the second or third year of life, clinicians are regularly asked to make diagnostic judgments about older children whom they are seeing for the first time. DSM-III-R now specifies autistic behaviors as manifest in older children and even adults, and the criteria can now be applied across a wider age range.

The chronic nature of Pervasive Developmental Disorder requires long-term treatment, and therapeutic goals should be directed toward specialized educational programs that encourage a degree of self-care and social functioning. Drug treatment is recommended only if it provides a reasonable level of improvement.

Focus on Autistic Disorder
Also called infantile autism or Kanner's syndrome, Autistic Disorder represents the current, although certainly not the final, step in a series of efforts to validate this subgrouping of profoundly disturbed children (Creak, 1964; GAP, 1974; Kanner, 1935; Ornitz & Ritvo, 1976; Rutter, 1978; Cohen et al., 1986). Autism is perhaps the childhood category best validated by empirical research. DSM-III-R defines specific behavioral criteria for disturbed social, communicative, motor, and intellectual behaviors usually acquired within the first three years of life.

Autistic Disorder was not included as a separate category in previous APA diagnostic manuals until DSM-III, although various sets of diagnostic criteria had been defined elsewhere (Creak, 1964; GAP, 1974; Kanner, 1935; Ornitz & Ritvo, 1976). DSM-III separated the category from its earlier association with psychosis and classified it as a Developmental Disorder, emphasizing the distortion of skills and functions that are normally acquired within the first 30 months of life. DSM-III-R retains this emphasis and specifies the qualitative impairment of developmental distortions in three areas: reciprocal social interaction, verbal and nonverbal communications skills, and imaginative activity. DSM-III-R drops onset of symptoms before 30 months of age as a diagnostic criterion, but childhood onset is specified if symptoms first occur after 36 months of age.

Qualitative impairment in reciprocal social interactions (formerly "lack of social responsiveness," DSM-III). Autistic Disorder, broadly defined, primarily describes an extreme social indifference and lack of responsiveness. This emphasis was established in the DSM-III criteria and is maintained in the revised edition. Clinicians now have a choice of behaviors reflecting social nonresponsiveness and for judging symptoms appearing after 30 months of age. As outlined in DSM-III-R, this feature includes a "lack of awareness of the existence or feeling of others," "no or abnormal seeking of comfort at times of distress," "no or impaired imitation," "no or abnormal social play," and "gross impairment in ability to make peer friendships." Defining impairment in this way avoids the difficulty in applying the DSM-III concept of "social-relatedness" in retrospective diagnosis of older children where superficial sociability may have been confused with apparent social-relatedness. Clinicians must still consider these issues when making retrospective diagnoses, but current criteria concerning social play and peer relations will help considerably in the evaluation of children above age three.

Infant and childhood nonresponsiveness can be manifested in the following ways:

- failure to cuddle
- lack of eye contact
- lack of facial expression
- indifference or aversion to affection/physical contact
- adults treated as interchangeable
- mechanical clinging to a specific adult
- failure to develop cooperative or imaginative play
- failure to develop friendships

Older children may attain a level of superficial sociability, such as:

- awareness of parents or familiar adults
- attachment to parents or familiar adults only, but failure to relate to others
- passive involvement in games or physical play

These abnormal social behaviors also tend to vary with age and the severity of the illness, although the deficit is exacerbated during interactions requiring initiative or reciprocal behaviors. Although the child may not withdraw from physical interactions such as rough-housing or tackling, he is unable to engage in imaginative play or participate in cooperative play. Whether or not this abnormality is a primary or secondary defect, it certainly is a pronounced feature. Autistic adolescents and adults continue to exhibit skill deficits and social inappropriateness in personal interactions.

Impairment in communications and imaginative activity (formerly "impaired ability to communicate," DSM-III). Both verbal and nonverbal areas of communication may be affected, and ability seems to vary according to stage of development and severity of the disorder. Language impairments can be evidenced in the degree of language development or in peculiar patterns of speech such as odd tone, volume, or pitch of speech; echolalia; or the use of neologisms. In some cases there may be no language at all, while in others language may be immature and minimal, lacking in spontaneity, or, in the higher-functioning patient, may be characterized by concreteness and nominal aphasia. Repetitive speech is also common, as are pronoun reversal and inability to use abstraction or metaphor. Some patients can readily decode written material, but show impairments in reading and comprehension. Nonverbal avenues of communication—gestures, facial expressions, and posture—are rarely used to compensate for impaired language abilities.

Play activity in most cases lacks imaginative content, is devoid of symbolic or fanciful behavior with toys or others, and shows marked absence of role-playing. Restricted in content, behavior is marked by a repetitive, stereotypical style.

Markedly restricted repertoire of activities and interests (formerly "bizarre responses to environment," DSM-III). Another characteristic of the autistic child is a restricted repertoire of behaviors and interests described as unusual and often bizarre responses to aspects of the environment. DSM-III-R gives more objective observable criteria for making this assessment. Such behaviors may consist of resistance or extreme negative reaction to minor environmental changes, ritualistic or compulsive behaviors and motor stereotypies, or attachments to certain objects. Typically, these behaviors are restricted to a relatively narrow repertoire of interests and activities. Such reactions tend to diminish with age, though they rarely disappear and may become more complex or organized. In older Pervasive Developmental Disorder children, such responses might be displayed by insistence on a precise routine, fascination with moving objects, verbal stereotypies, or repetition of information regardless of social context or appropriateness. This phenomenon has been explained as an adaptive response that is elicited because the child is unable to flexibly adapt to modifications in the environment and attempts to preserve what is known.

In spite of general agreement that Autistic Disorder and Schizophrenia are separate entities, there remains a puzzling subgroup of children who are impaired most severely in the area of thought process but who do not meet criteria for Schizophrenia. At present the boundaries, definition, and validity of the schizotypal and childhood schizophrenia concepts remain the topic of debate (Cantor et al., 1982; Green et al., 1984; Tanguay & Asarnow, 1985). Many of these children must be diagnosed as Pervasive Developmental Disorder Not Otherwise Specified in DSM-III-R. This is an area urgently awaiting further clarification.

Secondary Characteristics. Other characteristics commonly observed include cognitive impairment in the form of Mental Retardation or uneven development of specific skills; abnormal posturing and motor behaviors as well as poor coordination; odd responses to sensory input; abnormal eating, drinking, sleeping patterns; abnormal emotional responses such as mood lability, flat affect, excessive responses to unwarranted stimuli, generalized tension/anxiety; and self-injurious behaviors.

Diagnostic Issues

Diagnosis of Autistic Disorder in children with severe mental handicap. DSM-III-R does not give a lower IQ limit below which the diagnosis of Autistic Disorder should not be made. It is not clear if this was wise (and intellectual level should be specified for all cases in any circumstance). Because at least half of profoundly retarded children show some social and language impairment as well as repetitive behaviors some would argue that below, for example, an IQ of 35 the diagnosis should not be attempted. Because there was not full agreement on this point, however, no cutoff IQ was given. Most clinicians will still have considerable uncertainty on this point.

Autistic-like disorder in high-functioning children. As mentioned earlier, there remain several groups of children not satisfactorily categorized as either psychotic or autistic. Asperger's syndrome, for example (Wolff & Chick, 1980; Tantam, 1988), describes children of usually normal intelligence, with little empathy, odd communication patterns, and constricted and often rather odd interests. Whether these children have a mild form of Autistic Disorder or are best classified as having Schizoid Personality Disorder will be decided by research studies addressing follow-up, family, and associated features for such cases.

Autistic behavior in children with severe Developmental Language Disorders. Most children with Developmental Language Disorders can be readily differentiated from autistic children. But there are also children with behaviors and cognitive signs of both disorders. Research to date has not clarified this separation as well as one might wish, since in some cases of Autistic Disorder, family members have Developmental Language Disorder.

Further subtyping of Pervasive Developmental Disorder NOS. ICD-10 includes Childhood Disintegrative Disorder for a late-onset, Pervasive Developmental Disorder with clear signs of central nervous system disease (see Appendix I). It is argued that data are sufficiently strong for the validity of such a group, and that DSM-III-R also should have included it.

Recommendation. A recommendation for the future would be to add an IQ criterion to the diagnosis for Autistic Disorder, with provision for the assessment of nonverbal children with a standardized nonverbal measure. Best estimates indicate that only 40% of children with Autistic Disorder have IQ scores of less than 50. Extreme variability in intellectual functioning has been demonstrated within this diagnostic group. Other studies indicate that performance tends to be characteristically low for symbolic or abstract thought, while it may be good for manipulative or visual-spatial skills or rote memory. The presence of one or more areas of normal intellectual ability, despite subtest scatter, could also be added to the criteria.

Coding

Axis III. Associated physical disorders. Associated physical disorders should be coded on Axis III. Maternal rubella and fragile X syndrome are the most common. Epileptic seizures have been reported to develop in adolescence or adulthood in approximately 25% of those with the disorder; however, most children who developed seizures had IQ scores less than 50, while few with higher intelligence did. The coding of physical disorders is crucial, as Autistic Disorder is clearly a heterogeneous group for whom a variety of chromosomal metabolic and CNS abnormalities remain to be uncovered.

Axis IV. The chronic course of these disorders may have little responsiveness to social stressors per se. However, there is some evidence that those with higher ability levels may develop depression when they realize certain limitations due to their handicap. In addition, other symptom changes or exacerbations (i.e., catatonia, agitation, delusions, hallucinations, etc.) may be related to stress and often clear up rapidly when the source of the stress or stressor is removed.

Axis V. Highest level of adaptive functioning. Social awkwardness and ineptness persist even in residual state, and adequate social adjustment is primarily dependent on IQ and development of language skills.

Differential Diagnosis

Characteristic of Pervasive Developmental Disorder is a distorted development of multiple basic psychological functions involving the development of language and social skills such as attention, perception, and motor movement. The core disturbance affects many of these areas at the same time and to an abnormal degree. Initial diagnostic differences exist between these disorders, Mental Retardation, and Schizophrenia. In rare cases, rapid loss of language and social skills is secondary to central nervous system disease, whereas Pervasive Developmental Disorder is characterized by an initial abnormality in the development of such skills.

Schizophrenics may exhibit oddities of behavior similar to Pervasive Developmental Disorder, but there is also the presence of hallucinations, delusions, loosening of associations, or incoherence. None of the symptoms associated with impaired reality testing, as in Schizophrenia, are evident, although there may be presence of bizarre ideas and fantasies, preoccupation with morbid thoughts or interests, or pathological preoccupation with or attachment to objects.

In Schizotypal Personality Disorder, symptoms may exhibit similar oddities of behavior and speech, but the profound disturbance of social relations present in Pervasive Developmental Disorder is absent, language function is relatively intact, and there are no disturbances of motor movement, inappropriate affect, or self-mutilation.

There will remain a pool of patients with odd stilted personalities, constricted interests, subtly odd coordination patterns, and normal intelligence not yet well covered by any diagnostic scheme. Pervasive Developmental Disorder NOS awaits research to clarify further subgroups and set limits on level of functioning.

Deficits may be thought to be due to hearing impairment, and in the young infant an audiogram can easily determine whether this is the case. The hearing-impaired child will consistently respond to loud sounds whereas the autistic child's responses are inconsistent. Lack of responsiveness is sometimes difficult to assess in the youngster who has developed superficial skills or shows attachment behavior through continuous association with a caretaker. It is up to the clinician to establish his/her own guidelines for evaluating social relatedness, especially in an older child.

The autistic child retains such a pervasive lack of responsiveness that differential diagnosis of a child with Developmental Receptive Language Disorder is easily made by observing attempts to communicate through gesture, to make eye contact, and so forth.

Differentiation between Autistic Disorder and other disorders that show behavioral oddities depends on the extent to which other characteristic symptoms are present or absent, i.e., Pervasive Developmental Disorder Not Otherwise Specified, Schizotypal Personality Disorder, Schizophrenia, or Mental Retardation.

In Schizophrenia, evidence of psychotic features must be present for diagnosis. Also, no increased incidence of Schizophrenia is found in the familial histories of autistic children.

Mental Retardation is an additional diagnosis for some autistic children, as 40% are reported to have IQ scores less than 50. This issue needs future clarification. In some cases, it may be a matter of a test's inability to compute equivalent IQ scores for the nonverbal child; in others, the question is whether any distinction should be made if IQ is below 50. It may be helpful to note that the full autistic syndrome is rarely present in the child singularly diagnosed as mentally retarded.

299.80 Pervasive Developmental Disorder Not Otherwise Specified. This category is used when qualitative impairment is the same as in Autistic Disorder, but symptoms do not meet criteria for Autistic Disorder.

AXIS I: REACTIVE ATTACHMENT DISORDER OF INFANCY OR EARLY CHILDHOOD (313.89)

Reactive Attachment Disorder of Infancy is considered in the same chapter as Pervasive Developmental Disorder primarily because we felt that, for differential diagnosis, comparing it with a group of disorders encountered during the first years of life and encompassing developmental abnormalities was more appropriate than keeping it as an isolated subject. This disorder is coded on Axis I.

DSM-III-R not only specifies the behaviors indicative of defective or abnormal attachment, but also characterizes deficient caretaking situations most likely to be associated with the disorder.

By definition, Reactive Attachment Disorder of Infancy or Early Childhood is evidenced by impaired emotional and physical development prior to the age of five years and is directly attributable to grossly inadequate caretaking. Prominent deficits are failure to express age-appropriate signs of social responsiveness (or indiscriminate sociability) and failure to gain the expected amount of weight for the given age. The condition usually responds positively to nurturing and adequate care. It is not the result of a physical disorder, Mental Retardation, or Autistic

TABLE 12
313.89 Reactive Attachment Disorder of Infancy or Early Childhood: Diagnostic Criteria

A. Markedly disturbed social relatedness in most contexts, beginning before the age of five, as evidenced by either (1) or (2):
   1. persistent failure to initiate or respond to most social interactions (e.g., in infants, absence of visual tracking and reciprocal play, lack of vocal imitation or playfulness, apathy, little or no spontaneity; at later ages, lack of or little curiosity and social interest)
   2. indiscriminate sociability, e.g., excessive familiarity with relative strangers by making requests and displaying affection

B. The disturbance in A is not a symptom of either Mental Retardation or a Pervasive Developmental Disorder, such as Autistic Disorder.

C. Grossly pathogenic care, as evidenced by at least one of the following:
   1. persistent disregard of the child's basic emotional needs for comfort, stimulation, and affection (e.g., overly harsh punishment by caregiver; consistent neglect by caregiver)
   2. persistent disregard of the child's basic physical needs, including nutrition, adequate housing, and protection from physical danger and assault (including sexual abuse)
   3. repeated change of primary caregiver so that stable attachments are not possible (e.g., frequent changes in foster parents)

D. There is a presumption that the care described in C is responsible for the disturbed behavior in A; this presumption is warranted if the disturbance in A began following the pathogenic care in C.

Note: If failure to thrive is present, code it on Axis III.

Disorder. There may be cases in which Mental Retardation or Autistic Disorder would be diagnosed in addition to Reactive Attachment Disorder of Infancy or Early Childhood. The major distinction between these three conditions is that in Reactive Attachment Disorder there is medical evidence for extreme neglect which is directly responsible for this condition.

While DSM-III-R recognition of a syndrome that has an honorable tradition in child psychiatry research is a welcome gesture, some aspects of the diagnosis are bound to create problems. One difficulty, for instance, involves the continuing controversy which surrounds the age at which a diagnosis can and should be made. DSM-III-R states that this particular diagnosis can be made as early as in the first month of life. Another complication arises in that DSM-III-R suggests that interference in early emotional bonding is a predisposing factor in the condition, when it is difficult to establish with any objectivity that affectional bonds are actually formed in the infant.

Despite these issues, the definition of the disorder in DSM-III-R constitutes an improvement over DSM-III in a number of ways. The age of onset can be up to age five (not eight months as in DSM-III), which is much more in keeping with clinical experience and also avoids the debate over how early one can or must make a diagnosis of abnormal bonding in a group for whom delayed development is the rule.

In addition, the diagnosis is no longer defined in part by response to reinstatement of adequate caregiving. This was hardly a selective treatment in the first place, and such a criterion would obstruct research on how completely reversible Reactive Attachment Disorder truly is and whether some types are more treatable than others.

A continuing controversy is whether grossly pathogenic care should be part of the diagnostic definition. One argument against its inclusion is that research has not yet established how frequently such a syndrome can occur in the *absence* of grossly defective care. When the nature of the care is a defining feature, then, as Rutter has pointed out (1988), the association between the child syndrome and environmental circumstances cannot be investigated.

CASE HISTORIES

Jason
Jason is an attractive five-and-a-half-year-old youngster who shows significant delays in social and self-help skills. He makes sounds but as yet

has not formed words. At times he engages in peculiar finger movements and will flap his hands when he is either very happy or angry. His parents report that sometimes he is fleetingly cuddly, but he does not play appropriately or tolerate other children very well. Inappropriate behaviors make him a management problem, and he often has temper tantrums and screams without cause. He does not react to spankings and if injured does not cry. His minor daily rituals are tolerated by his family, but interruptions cause him considerable distress. At this point he does not yet dress himself and wears diapers day and night. He is very attached to a stuffed teddy bear but easily separates from his mother. Often he will engross himself for long periods twirling a tissue or blades of grass in front of his face. His parents are concerned that his obliviousness to danger may cause him harm unless he is constantly supervised. They report that he rarely complies with expected tasks.

Jason was 18 months old when his parents began to suspect that he was different. He seemed "too good" and, at the same time, not responsive enough. A hearing evaluation was normal. Intellectual functioning could not be accurately assessed, but the examiner felt there was some impairment.

On a recent clinic visit Jason continued to display poor social relatedness and very superficial skills. He easily took the interviewer's hand and did not seem to discriminate between his mother and strangers. An occasional grimace momentarily altered his somewhat bland expression, and he appeared tuned out and disinterested in most things about him. The background noise in the clinic agitated him, and he frequently put his fingers in his ears. When he was upset, he butted his head against his mother and resisted tactile contact.

Diagnosis

Axis I:	299.00 Autistic Disorder
Axis II:	317.00 Mild Mental Retardation (Provisional)
Axis III:	None
Axis IV:	Severity: 1—None
	Stressors: N/A
Axis V:	Current GAF: 20
	Highest GAF past year: 30

Discussion

Jason exhibits the characteristic symptoms of Autistic Disorder. The early onset (before 36 months) and Jason's lack of responsiveness, odd behaviors, and absent language make this diagnosis straightforward. It is important that the observer rate relatedness, however, as parents often offer their own interpretation of the child's interactions, which may not agree with the child's relatedness as seen by others. Evaluation of intellectual functioning was not helpful, but even a crude assessment of intellectual level is useful for treatment planning. While the Axis V assessments reflect Jason's inability to function in most areas and his gross impairment in communication skills, there is some question as to the meaningfulness of these ratings and whether they can be adapted for childhood disorders and also take developmental abnormalities into account.

Helen

Helen, an eight-month-old, was referred by her caseworker before placement in foster care. She was in the 15th percentile for weight, although length was normal. The caseworker was struck by Helen's sad expression and lack of interest in toys or visitors. Her existence had been chaotic since birth. Born to a chronic paranoid schizophrenic mother, who was now reinstitutionalized, her father unknown, Helen had had minimal care from her mother and only begrudging ministrations from a landlady who had taken tenuous claim of her with the exacerbation of the mother's illness. The mother had been hallucinating and delusional since Helen's birth, and it was doubtful whether she would ever be able to provide the adequate care the infant needed. During the examination, Helen was apathetic and disinterested in the examiner. She made no sounds. Motor development was normal.

Six months after placement in a foster home, Helen's weight had increased to the 50th percentile, she had begun to exhibit a few signs of responsiveness toward the foster mother, and she vocalized some sounds. She was fearful, however, and cried periodically without apparent cause.

Diagnosis

>Axis I: 313.89 Reactive Attachment Disorder of Infancy
>Axis II: V71.09 No diagnosis on Axis II
>Axis III: None
>Axis IV: Severity: 6—Extreme (predominantly enduring circumstances)
>   Stressors: Mental illness in parent; gross neglect; lack of consistent caretaker
>Axis V: Current GAF: 55
>   Highest GAF past year: Not applicable

Discussion

Evidence of the disorder is confirmed by medical examination. There is history of neglect. Partial improvement of symptoms shows response to more favorable conditions. It seems unlikely, however, that Helen can achieve complete recovery from these disastrous circumstances, and she may already qualify for a second diagnosis of Major Depression. Environmental circumstances may play a major role in treatment planning.

Axis IV would be more useful if particular stressors were given severity codes. Note that Axis V as used in the British system (see Appendix I) would be most helpful—a code of 01—Mental Disturbance in Other Family Members. This case illustrates the relative uselessness of Axis V for many childhood cases. The DSM-III-R Axis V, highest level of functioning, is most applicable for disorders that are rarely diagnosed in childhood.

Chapter 10

Schizophrenia and Other Disorders with Psychotic Features

Schizophrenia is primarily a disorder of young adulthood and for this reason has not been included in the DSM-III-R section on Disorders Usually First Evident in Infancy, Childhood, or Adolescence. However, its relatively frequent occurrence in late adolescence, as well as the considerable debate about the use of this diagnosis for children, prompts further discussion of the application of this definition in pediatric diagnosis.

DSM-III-R DEFINITION OF SCHIZOPHRENIA

Use of the Term "Psychotic"
DSM-III-R clearly defines subtypes of Schizophrenia and carefully distinguishes them from other disorders. A primary concept is the term "psychotic," which describes a broad range of behaviors marked by gross impairment in reality testing. The term can be applied to behavior or can indicate the phase of a disorder in which the behavior occurs. When this condition exists, the individual is unable to correctly evaluate the accuracy of his/her perceptions and thoughts and therefore makes incorrect assumptions about external reality. Evidence of this process in Schizophrenia is characterized by delusions or hallucinations, grossly disorganized behavior, or incoherent speech. The specific symptoms cited in

DSM-III-R criteria for Schizophrenia are characterized by disruption of numerous psychological functions. Specified psychotic symptoms must be present for at least one week during the active phase of the illness in order to diagnose Schizophrenia. (For a complete account, see the section on Schizophrenia, pp. 187–198, of the DSM-III-R.)

Psychotic characteristics are evident in disorders other than Schizophrenia and imply impaired reality testing. In DSM-III-R, psychotic disorders include Paranoid Disorders, some Mood Disorders and Organic Mental Disorders, and Psychotic Disorders Not Elsewhere Classified. Within each of these categories there are specific guidelines concerning the nature of the psychotic features; these guidelines must be closely observed for differential diagnosis. This subtle distinction is important for diagnostic differentiation between psychotic disturbance and Mental Retardation or Pervasive Developmental Disorder within the pediatric age group. Unfortunately, there is no separate coding for childhood onset of Schizophrenia. But Schizophrenia preempts a diagnosis of Pervasive Developmental Disorder if both are thought to exist.

TABLE 13
Schizophrenia: Diagnostic Criteria

A. Presence of characteristic psychotic symptoms in the active phase: either (1), (2), or (3) for at least one week (unless the symptoms are successfully treated):
    1. Two of the following:
        (a) delusions
        (b) prominent hallucinations (throughout the day for several days or several times a week for several weeks, each hallucinatory experience not being limited to a few brief moments)
        (c) incoherence or marked loosening of associations
        (d) catatonic behavior
        (e) flat or grossly inappropriate affect
    2. Bizarre delusions (i.e., involving a phenomenon that the person's culture would regard as totally implausible, e.g., thought broadcasting, being controlled by a dead person)
    3. Prominent hallucinations [as defined in (1)(b) above] of a voice with content having no apparent relation to depression or elation, or a voice keeping up a running commentary on the person's behavior or thoughts, or two or more voices conversing with each other

B. During the course of the disturbance, functioning in such areas as work, social relations, and self-care is markedly below the highest level achieved

Differential Diagnosis

The DSM-III-R clinical criteria for Schizophrenia include a characteristic symptom picture encompassing social and occupational functioning in which the clinical course follows a typical pattern with a minimum six-month duration (see Table 13).

If duration is less than one month and in response to a stressor, a diagnosis of Brief Reactive Psychosis is considered. Duration of more than two weeks but less than six months is considered Schizophreniform Disorder. (No minimal duration—instead code prognosis.) In the event that the latter two disorders, which are exactly the same as Schizophrenia except for duration, should extend past the specified duration time, the diagnosis would change accordingly to Schizophrenia.

Diagnosis of a Mood Disorder should take precedence if there is a prominent disturbance of mood prior to onset of psychotic features. When this differentiation is too difficult to determine, the category of Schizoaffective Disorder may be indicated.

With adolescents especially, it is important to rule out a Substance-

---

TABLE 13 *(continued)*

---

before onset of the disturbance (or, when the onset is in childhood or adolescence, failure to achieve expected level of social development).

C. Schizoaffective Disorder and Mood Disorder with Psychotic Features have been ruled out; i.e., if a Major Depressive or Manic Syndrome has ever been present during an active phase of the disturbance, the total duration of all episodes of a mood syndrome has been brief relative to the total duration of the active and residual phases of the disturbance.

D. Continuous signs of the disturbance for at least six months. The six-month period must include an active phase (of at least one week, or less if symptoms have been successfully treated) during which there were psychotic symptoms characteristic of Schizophrenia (symptoms in A), with or without a prodromal or residual phase, as defined below.

   Prodromal phase: A clear deterioration in functioning before the active phase of the disturbance that is not due to a disturbance in mood or to a Psychoactive Substance Use Disorder and that involves at least two of the symptoms listed below.

   Residual phase: Following the active phase of the disturbance, persistence of at least two of the symptoms noted below, these not

(continued)

TABLE 13 *(continued)*

being due to a disturbance in mood or to a Psychoactive Substance Use
Disorder.

Prodromal or Residual Symptoms:

1. marked social isolation or withdrawal
2. marked impairment in role functioning as wage earner, student, or
   homemaker
3. markedly peculiar behavior (e.g., collecting garbage, talking to self in
   public, hoarding food)
4. marked impairment in personal hygiene and grooming
5. blunted or inappropriate affect
6. digressive, vague, overelaborate, or circumstantial speech, or poverty
   of speech, or poverty of content of speech
7. odd beliefs or magical thinking, influencing behavior and inconsistent
   with cultural norms (e.g., superstitiousness, belief in clairvoyance,
   telepathy, "sixth sense," "others can feel my feelings," overvalued
   ideas, ideas of reference)

Induced Organic Delusional Syndrome, especially during an initial, flor-
idly psychotic episode. Duration will also be important for differentiation,
although substance abuse may be a precipitating factor in the onset of a
more serious condition.

If Mental Retardation is present, Schizophrenia can be diagnosed
only if there are sufficient symptoms present that are not accounted for by
retardation, in which case a multiple diagnosis is appropriate.

If systematically organized persecutory or jealous delusions are present but there is no other evidence of hallucinations or more bizarre
delusions or disordered thinking, a diagnosis of a Paranoid Disorder is
considered. Paranoid Disorders feature an organized delusional system in
an otherwise more or less intact individual and are not usually diagnosed
in younger children. In Delusional (Paranoid) Disorder, the marked drop
in level of functioning that is necessary for the diagnosis of Schizophrenia
does not usually occur.

The DSM-III-R category Psychotic Disorders Not Elsewhere Classified includes Brief Reactive Psychosis, Schizophreniform Disorder,
Schizoaffective Disorder, Induced Psychotic Disorder, and Psychotic Disorders Not Otherwise Specified. These are of little importance for consideration in childhood diagnosis, with the exception of Schizophreniform
Disorder, which may occur with some frequency in adolescence. These

TABLE 13 *(continued)*

8. unusual perceptual experiences (e.g., recurrent illusions, sensing the presence of a force or person not actually present)
9. marked lack of initiative, interests, or energy

Examples: Six months of prodromal symptoms with one week of symptoms from A; no prodromal symptoms with six months of symptoms from A; no prodromal symptoms with one week of symptoms from A and six months of residual symptoms.

E. It cannot be established that an organic factor initiated and maintained the disturbance.

F. If there is a history of Autistic Disorder, the additional diagnosis of Schizophrenia is made only if prominent delusions or hallucinations are also present.

and other differential diagnoses are discussed more extensively in DSM-III-R, which should be consulted if necessary. They include:

- Organic Mental Disorders
- Organic Delusional Syndromes
- Mood Disorders (Depressive Disorder Not Otherwise Specified, Bipolar Disorder Not Otherwise Specified, Mood Disorder with Psychotic Features)
- Obsessive Compulsive Disorder
- Hypochondriasis
- Personality Disorders (Schizotypal, Borderline, Schizoid, Paranoid)
- Delusional Disorder (specified by type)
- Induced Psychotic Disorder
- Factitious Disorder with Psychological Symptoms

Coding

Axis II. Record premorbid personality disorder if known. Follow coding with (Premorbid).

TABLE 14
Schizophrenia: DSM-III-R Axis I Codes

295.1x	Disorganized Type
295.2x	Catatonic Type
295.3x	Paranoid Type
295.9x	Undifferentiated Type
295.6x	Residual Type

Fifth digit codes classify course of the illness:

1 *Subchronic.* More or less continuous signs of the illness, including prodromal, active, and residual phases, are apparent for at least six months but less than two years.
2 *Chronic.* Same course as above for more than two years.
3 *Subchronic with Acute Exacerbation.* Residual phase is followed by recurrence of prominent psychotic symptoms in subchronic course.
4 *Chronic with Acute Exacerbation. Residual phase is followed by recurrence of prominent psychotic symptoms in chronic course.*
5 *In Remission.* Used when individual no longer displays signs of illness for a period of time.
0 Unspecified.

      Axis IV. Record any psychosocial stressor that may have been associated with onset.

      Axis V. Record previous level of functioning for one year and current level using GAF. One often sees deterioration from previous level in areas of functioning such as performance of expected duties, social relations, and self-care or failure to achieve expected level of social development (in onset in childhood or adolescence).

USE OF THE DIAGNOSIS WITH CHILDREN
In DSM-II, "childhood schizophrenia" was the only category referring to psychotic disorders of childhood. DSM-III and now DSM-III-R categories include the Pervasive Developmental Disorders as well as Schizophrenia, which is not particularly distinguished for children. DSM-III-R seeks to make a clear distinction between Schizophrenia and Autistic Disorder, on the assumption that the best available evidence indicates that they are two distinct disorders (Rutter & Schopler, 1978).

TABLE 15
Schizophrenia Subtypes: Essential Features

a. **Disorganized:** Incoherence and flat or inappropriate affect, accompanied by associated oddities of behavior and social impairment, are considered the most prominent features of this type of Schizophrenia. Onset is typically early and insidious with a chronic course.

b. **Catatonic:** The most striking thing about this subtype is psychomotor disturbance. Mutism is also common. Occurrence of this subtype is now rare.

c. **Paranoid:** This subtype is marked by the prominence of one or more systematized delusions or auditory hallucinations related to a recurrent theme. A person with this disorder is likely to be argumentative and at times violent; he/she may show generalized anxiety. (Doubts of gender identity are commonly expressed.) In Paranoid Disorders, the delusions are more systematized and believable and there is absence of hallucinations, thought disorder, or disoriented behaviors. Absence: incoherence, loose associations, flat or inappropriate affect or disorganized behavior characteristics of the former two types. Specify if stable type.

d. **Undifferentiated:** Prominent psychotic symptoms that cannot be classified in any of the other subtypes or that meet more than one of the subtypes.

e. **Residual:** This code is used when the patient is without prominent psychotic symptoms, but signs of the illness persist as indicated by presence of two or more of the residual symptoms listed in the diagnostic criteria for Schizophrenia.

In childhood, Schizophrenia is less clearly differentiated by separate subtypes. Kanner (1962) emphasized, for example, that there is less content and less variability clinically than with adult patients; he focused instead on emotional withdrawal, diminished interest in the environment, alterations in motility patterns, and perseverations or stereotypy. There is considerable debate about the manifestation of Schizophrenia specific to childhood. Some writers (e.g., Cantor et al., 1982) argue for validity of a separate category of childhood schizophrenia, suggesting that these children have age-specific impairments of the motor system, that the disorder can be manifest even before 36 months of age, and that abnormal thought processes and content become manifest between the ages of three and five, when appropriate language development should occur.

**Differentiation Between Schizophrenia and
Pervasive Developmental Disorder**
In practice, DSM-III-R deals with this controversial problem in the most
straightforward way. The best validated category, that of Autistic Disorder,
is clearly defined by pervasive lack of responsiveness and gross deficits in
language development. Furthermore, there must be a lack of delusions,
hallucinations, loosening of associations, and incoherences, which clearly
distinguish it from Schizophrenia, and onset of Pervasive Developmental
Disorder usually occurs at an early age. There remains some controversy
around this distinction, however, as Fish (1977) argues for continuity
between the conditions. The DSM-III category of Pervasive Developmental Disorder, Childhood-Onset is a subtype about which the least is
known. In DSM-III-R, this disorder is no longer treated as a separate
category but is coded within Autistic Disorder.

The essential features (see section in Chapter 9 on Pervasive Developmental Disorder) emphasize gross impairment in social relationships and
major impairment in the development of multiple basic psychological
functions. The relationship between Pervasive Developmental Disorder,
as defined in DSM-III-R, and the disorder of childhood schizophrenia proposed by Cantor and others (1982) is unclear. However, by providing clear
definitions, DSM-III-R provides the tools for empirically testing the validity of the category. A follow-up study of a group of children so defined has
yet to be undertaken. If DSM-III-R had provided a separate coding for
childhood onset of Schizophrenia, such research would be facilitated.

In practice, difficulties may frequently arise when clinicians are faced
with the atypical case or with children between the ages of three and
seven. A pragmatic task for clinicians is to decide whether or not a
diagnosis of thought disorder can be made or how presence or absence of
hallucinations and delusions should be assessed in the nonverbal child. If
a nonverbal child appears to be watching something on the ceiling, for
example, when the examiner can see nothing, should the diagnosis of
visual hallucinations be made? Similarly, how can one assess cognitive
incoherence in children with speech abnormalities? Unless thought disorder,
hallucinations, or delusions can be shown without a doubt, it is suggested
that Pervasive Developmental Disorder Not Otherwise Specified be diagnosed in young children (i.e., onset before age 12).

Differentiation from Other Categories
DSM-III-R eliminated the separate category of Schizoid Disorder of Childhood or Adolescence on the basis that this was quite similar to Schizoid

Personality Disorder. When differentiating the disorders discussed above from Schizoid Personality Disorder, the clinician should note that the latter classification is reserved for those with social isolation of a consistent and chronic nature, who do not have formal thought disorder or show the deterioration seen in Schizophrenia or any other psychotic disorder. The diagnosis of Schizoid Personality Disorder is more easily distinguished from Avoidant Disorder of Childhood or Adolescence because in the latter condition social relations within the family are considered normal and satisfying and the withdrawal occurs on the basis of anxiety. There has been virtually no consideration of Schizotypal Personality Disorder, but in its new form in DSM-III-R, it is distinguished from Schizoid Personality Disorder by the display of odd behaviors, thinking, perception, and speech. Since there is no acute type of Schizophrenia and diagnosis requires six months' duration, Schizophreniform Disorder should be used.

SCHIZOPHRENIFORM DISORDER

The features of this disorder are identical with those of Schizophrenia with the exception that duration, including the prodromal, active, and residual phases, is less than six months. This category was modified in

---

TABLE 16
295.40 Schizophreniform Disorder: Diagnostic Criteria

A. Meets criteria A and C of Schizophrenia

B. An episode of the disturbance (including prodromal, active, and residual phases) lasts less than six months. (When the diagnosis must be made without waiting for recovery, it should be qualified as "provisional.")

C. Does not meet the criteria for Brief Reactive Psychosis, and it cannot be established that an organic factor initiated and maintained the disturbance.

Specify: without good prognostic features or with good prognostic features, i.e., with at least two of the following:
   1. onset of prominent psychotic symptoms within four weeks of first noticeable change in usual behavior or functioning
   2. confusion, disorientation, or perplexity at the height of the psychotic episode
   3. good premorbid social and occupational functioning
   4. absence of blunted or flat affect

DSM-III-R to reflect features that have been identified with a relatively good prognosis. In instances where a person is symptomatic for six months and whose course continues, the diagnosis is changed to the appropriate Schizophrenia subtype and coded "Provisional." The clinical picture of this disorder is most often characterized by emotional turmoil, fear, confusion, and vivid hallucinations.

CASE HISTORIES

Stephen
Stephen, age 15, had been a good student, played chess and checkers, and kept a garden in the family suburban home. His mother was very controlling toward all the children and required them to spend a lot of their free time visiting her elderly relatives. She and Stephen's father, a rather withdrawn man, disagreed openly about childrearing and most other subjects. Stephen's older sister had emancipated herself after a violent, probably irrevocable break with the family. Stephen had always wet the bed at least once a week, which was painfully embarrassing to him.

Since age 12, Stephen had avoided all companions. At age 14, however, he received honorable mention in school because of a paper he wrote tracing his ancestors back 10 generations, discussing the importance of knowing one's roots. He was not pleased with the attention and stopped going to school. Over the following 10 months, Stephen became progressively bizarre, keeping notebooks in the cellar and wondering if there were ancestors buried there. His parents had been proud of his scholarship but finally became alarmed when he began to dig in the cellar looking for traces of these early burials.

By the time he was 15, Stephen had gradually become more silent and developed odd jerks of the head and chewing movements of the jaw. His family finally sent him to a state hospital where he became mute, soiling and sometimes smearing feces.

Diagnosis
Axis I:	295.92 Schizophrenia, Undifferentiated
	307.60 Functional Enuresis, Primary
Axis II:	301.22 Schizotypal Personality Disorder (Premorbid)
Axis III:	None

Axis IV: Severity: 4—Moderate (predominantly enduring
circumstances)
Stressor(s): Family discord
Axis V: Current GAF: 15
Highest GAF past year: 20

Discussion

Initially Stephen met diagnostic criteria for Schizotypal Personality Disorder.
His normal language and early development ruled out a diagnosis of
Pervasive Developmental Disorder. The disintegration of and defects in
Stephen's reality testing as well as the development of delusions, then
mutism, meet the criteria for Schizophrenia. The fifth-digit code indicates
a subchronic course since symptoms have persisted more than six months
but less than two years.

Again, use of the British Axis V (02.—Discordant Intrafamilial Relationships; see Appendix I) would be useful and important for treatment
planning. Note that Primary Enuresis (also Axis I) predated the present
illness and is one of a group of developmental delays slightly more
common in high-risk children. The odd motor movements are common in
Schizophrenia and do not warrant any additional coding.

Schizotypal Personality Disorder (as in Stephen's case) may eventually be a useful category for documenting bizarre schizophrenic-like
thought processes in childhood. When making a differential diagnosis
between Schizotypal Personality Disorder and Pervasive Developmental Disorder NOS, the Personality Disorder takes precedence unless deficits exist that are totally attributable to the Pervasive Developmental
Disorder. These distinctions need further clarification for child psychiatric classification.

Evan

Evan is a 16-year-old, exceptionally good student, particularly in math
and science. His parents, however, have been concerned since he was six or
seven about his extreme social isolation and lack of affection. During
grade school, he constructed a shortwave radio and spent most of his free
time perfecting the design and listening to foreign stations. He became
very interested in following the weather reports of different countries.

His recent fascination is satellite photographs of weather conditions
around the world. In addition, Evan spends much time phoning various

weather services and subscribes to several meteorological publications. He enjoys discussing the topic, but has little awareness of whether or not his audience is also interested. One or two friends briefly shared this interest, but have since dropped off and become interested in school activities.

Evan is emotionless and polite. Occasionally he expresses irritation over his parents' attempts to "interfere" in his affairs, though basically he considers them to be on his side, particularly his mother. Although he has no interest in sports, he is well coordinated and has no peculiarities of movement. He hopes to work at a weather station when he grows up and is particularly interested in working in the Antarctic.

Diagnosis

Axis I:	V71.09 No diagnosis on Axis I	
Axis II:	301.20 Schizoid Personality Disorder	
Axis III:	None	
Axis IV:	Severity: 1—None	
	Stressor(s): N/A	
Axis V:	Current GAF: 55	
	Highest GAF past year: 60	

Discussion

The flavor of Evan's clinical picture is more descriptive of a personality style than of more severe disorders. Since this pattern has been stable for some time, a diagnosis of Schizoid Personality Disorder is appropriate, reflecting the aloof, isolated nature of Evan's social interactions. Evan's development as an infant was normal and his cognitive and language functioning developed normally; therefore, he does not fit criteria for Pervasive Developmental Disorder. There are undoubtedly high-functioning autistic children who are elsewhere described as having Asperger's syndrome (see discussion in Chapter 9) and who would resemble Evan in personality. The presence of cognitive defects or uneven language skills would be distinctive for Pervasive Developmental Disorder.

There is no evidence of disturbance of thought, delusions, or hallucinations, which rules out Schizophrenia. Evan is irritable at times when disturbed, but has none of the antisocial behaviors that would be characteristic of Conduct Disorder and is, in fact, singularly honest and reliable within the limitations of his social abilities. At this point in Evan's life, the time-honored diagnosis of Schizoid Personality seems most appropriate.

Chapter 11

Mood Disorders

DSM-III-R DEFINITION OF MOOD DISORDERS

A diagnosis of a Mood Disorder presupposes a primary disturbance of mood manifested by excessively high or low mood states that occur together for a minimal duration of time. Associated symptoms are not attributed to any other physical or mental disorder. DSM-III-R groups these disorders under two basic categories: Bipolar Disorder and Depressive Disorders.

The DSM-III-R criteria for Major Depressive Episode and Manic Episode are summarized in Tables 17 and 18.

TABLE 17
Major Depressive Episode: Diagnostic Criteria

Note: A "Major Depressive Syndrome" is defined as criterion A below.

A. At least five of the following symptoms have been present during the same two-week period and represent a change from previous functioning; at least one of the symptoms is either (1) depressed mood, or (2) loss of interest or pleasure. (Do not include symptoms that are clearly due to a physical condition, mood-incongruent delusions or hallucinations, incoherence, or marked loosening of associations.)
   1. Depressed mood (or can be irritable mood in children and adolescents) most of the day, nearly every day, as indicated either by subjective account or observation by others

(continued)

95

TABLE 17 *(continued)*

2.   Markedly diminished interest or pleasure in all, or almost all, activities most of the day, nearly every day (as indicated either by subjective account or observation by others of apathy most of the time)
3.   Significant weight loss or weight gain when not dieting (e.g., more than 5% of body weight in a month), or decrease or increase in appetite nearly every day (in children, consider failure to make expected weight gains)
4.   Insomnia or hypersomnia nearly every day
5.   Psychomotor agitation or retardation nearly every day (observable by others, not merely subjective feelings of restlessness or being slowed down)
6.   Fatigue or loss of energy nearly every day
7.   Feelings of worthlessness or excessive or inappropriate guilt (which may be delusional) nearly every day (not merely self-reproach or guilt about being sick)
8.   Diminished ability to think or concentrate, or indecisiveness, nearly every day (either by subjective account or as observed by others)
9.   Recurrent thoughts of death (not just fear of dying), recurrent suicidal ideation without a specific plan, or a suicide attempt or a specific plan for committing suicide

B.   1.   It cannot be established that an organic factor initiated and maintained the disturbance.
    2.   The disturbance is not a normal reaction to the death of a loved one (Uncomplicated Bereavement).
        Note: Morbid preoccupation with worthlessness, suicidal idea-tion, marked functional impairment or psychomotor retardation, or prolonged duration suggest bereavement complicated by Major Depression.

C.   At no time during the disturbance have there been delusions or hallucinations for as long as two weeks in the absence of prominent mood symptoms (i.e., before the mood symptoms developed or after they have remitted).

D.   Not superimposed on Schizophrenia, Schizophreniform Disorder, Delu-sional Disorder, or Psychotic Disorder NOS.

Specify chronic if current episode has lasted two consecutive years without a period of two months or longer during which there were no significant depressive symptoms.
Specify if current episode is **Melancholic Type.**

TABLE 18
Manic Episode: Diagnostic Criteria

Note: A "Manic Syndrome" is defined as including criteria A, B, and C below. A "Hypomanic Syndrome" is defined as including criteria A and B, but not C, i.e., no marked impairment.

A. A distinct period of abnormally and persistently elevated, expansive, or irritable mood.

B. During the period of mood disturbance, at least three of the following symptoms have persisted (four if the mood is only irritable) and have been present to a significant degree:
    1. inflated self-esteem or grandiosity
    2. decreased need for sleep (e.g., feels rested after only three hours of sleep)
    3. more talkative than usual or pressure to keep talking
    4. flight of ideas or subjective experience that thoughts are racing
    5. distractibility (i.e., attention too easily drawn to unimportant or irrelevant external stimuli)
    6. increase in goal-directed activity (either socially, at work or school, or sexually) or psychomotor agitation
    7. excessive involvement in pleasurable activities that have a high potential for painful consequences (e.g., the person engages in unrestrained buying sprees, sexual indiscretions, or foolish business investments)

C. Mood disturbance sufficiently severe to cause marked impairment in occupational functioning or in usual social activities or relationships with others, or to necessitate hospitalization to prevent harm to self or others.

D. At no time during the disturbance have there been delusions or hallucinations for as long as two weeks in the absence of prominent mood symptoms (i.e., before the mood symptoms developed or after they have remitted).

E. Not superimposed on Schizophrenia, Schizophreniform Disorder, Delusional Disorder, or Psychotic Disorder NOS.

F. It cannot be established that an organic factor initiated and maintained the disturbance.

Note: Somatic antidepressant treatment (e.g., drugs, ECT) that apparently precipitates a mood disturbance should not be considered an etiological organic factor.

TABLE 19
Mood Disorders: DSM-III-R Axis I Codes

Bipolar Disorders
(For fifth-digit codes, use Manic Episode codes to describe current state)
296.6x   Bipolar Disorder, Mixed
296.4x   Bipolar Disorder, Manic
296.5x   Bipolar Disorder, Depressed
296.70   Bipolar Disorder Not Otherwise Specified

　　　　Specify if seasonal pattern

Depressive Disorders
(For fifth-digit codes, use Major Depressive Episode codes to describe current state)
296.2x   Major Depression, Single Episode
296.3x   Major Depression, Recurrent
311.00   Depressive Disorder Not Otherwise Specified

　　　　Specify if seasonal pattern

301.13   Cyclothymia

300.40   Dysthymia

　　　　Specify if early or late onset

Fifth-digit codes for Major Depressive Episode and for Manic Episode
　　1   Mild
　　2   Moderate
　　3   Severe, without psychotic features
　　4   With psychotic features
　　　　Specify mood-congruent psychotic features or mood-incongruent
　　　　psychotic features
　　6   In full remission
　　0   Unspecified

Essential Features and Differential Diagnosis of Mood Disorders
The basic difference between Bipolar Disorders and Depressive Disorders is that in the former there is an occurrence of both a Major Depressive Episode and a Manic Episode (see Tables 20 and 21). Cyclothymia and Dysthymia have symptoms characteristic of the manic and depressive syndromes but have different criteria for severity and duration (see Tables 22 and 23). Bipolar Disorder Not Otherwise Specified and Depressive Disorder Not Otherwise Specified are residual categories provided for those instances when manic or depressive features do not meet the clinical guidelines established for the other Mood Disorders.

TABLE 20
Bipolar Disorders: Diagnostic Criteria

296.6x   Bipolar Disorder, Mixed
For fifth digit, use the Manic Episode codes to describe current state.
A.   Current (or most recent) episode involves the full symptomatic picture of both Manic and Major Depressive Episodes (except for the duration requirement of two weeks for depressive symptoms), intermixed or rapidly alternating every few days.
B.   Prominent depressive symptoms last at least a full day.

Specify if seasonal pattern.

296.4x   Bipolar Disorder, Manic
For fifth digit, use the Manic Episode codes to describe current state.
Currently (or most recently) in a Manic Episode. (If there has been a previous Manic Episode, the current episode need not meet the full criteria for a Manic Episode.)

296.5x   Bipolar Disorder, Depressed
For fifth digit, use the Major Depressive Episode codes to describe current state.
A.   Has had one or more Manic Episodes.
B.   Currently (or most recently) in a Major Depressive Episode. (If there has been a previous Major Depressive Episode, the current episode need not meet the full criteria for a Major Depressive Episode.)

Specify if seasonal pattern.

TABLE 21
Major Depression: Diagnostic Criteria

296.2x   Major Depression, Single Episode
For fifth digit, use the Major Depressive Episode codes to describe current state.
A.   A single Major Depressive Episode.
B.   Has never had a Manic Episode or an unequivocal Hypomanic Episode.

Specify if seasonal pattern.

296.3x   Major Depression, Recurrent
For fifth digit, use the Major Depressive Episode codes to describe current state.
A.   Two or more Major Depressive Episodes, each separated by at least two months of return to more or less usual functioning. (If there has been a previous Major Depressive Episode, the current episode of depression need not meet the full criteria for a Major Depressive Episode.)
B.   Has never had a Manic Episode or an unequivocal Hypomanic Episode.

Specify if seasonal pattern.

TABLE 22
300.40 Dysthymia: Diagnostic Criteria

A. Depressed mood (or can be irritable mood in children and adolescents) for most of the day, more days than not, as indicated either by subjective account or observation by others, for at least two years (one year for children and adolescents).

B. Presence, while depressed, of at least two of the following:
    1. poor appetite or overeating
    2. insomnia or hypersomnia
    3. low energy or fatigue
    4. low self-esteem
    5. poor concentration or difficulty making decisions
    6. feelings of hopelessness

C. During a two-year period (one year for children and adolescents) of the disturbance, never without the symptoms in A for more than two months at a time.

D. No evidence of an unequivocal Major Depressive Episode during the first two years (one year for children and adolescents) of the disturbance.
    Note: There may have been a previous Major Depressive Episode, provided there was a full remission (no significant signs or symptoms for six months) before development of the Dysthymia. In addition, after these two years (one year in children or adolescents) of Dysthymia, there may be superimposed episodes of Major Depression, in which case both diagnoses are given.

E. Has never had a Manic Episode or an unequivocal Hypomanic Episode.

F. Not superimposed on a chronic psychotic disorder, such as Schizophrenia or Delusional Disorder.

G. It cannot be established that an organic factor initiated and maintained the disturbance (e.g., prolonged administration of an antihypertensive medication).

Specify primary or secondary type.
   Primary type: the mood disturbance is not related to a preexisting, chronic, nonmood, Axis I or Axis III disorder (e.g., Anorexia Nervosa, Somatization Disorder, a Psychoactive Substance Dependence Disorder, an Anxiety Disorder, or rheumatoid arthritis).
   Secondary type: the mood disturbance is apparently related to a preexisting, chronic, nonmood Axis I or Axis III disorder.

Specify early onset or late onset.
   Early onset: onset of the disturbance before age 21.
   Late onset: onset of the disturbance at age 21 or later.

TABLE 23
301.13 Cyclothymia: Diagnostic Criteria

A. ·For at least two years (one year for children and adolescents), presence of numerous Hypomanic Episodes (all of the criteria for a Manic Episode except criterion C that indicates marked impairment) and numerous periods with depressed mood or loss of interest or pleasure that did not meet criterion A of Major Depressive Episode.

B. During a two-year period (one year in children and adolescents) of the disturbance, never without hypomanic or depressive symptoms for more than two months at a time.

C. No clear evidence of a Major Depressive Episode or Manic Episode during the first two years of the disturbance (or one year in children and adolescents).
    Note: After this minimum period of Cyclothymia, there may be superimposed Manic or Major Depressive Episodes, in which case the additional diagnosis of Bipolar Disorder or Bipolar Disorder NOS should be given.

D. Not superimposed on a chronic psychotic disorder, such as Schizophrenia or Delusional Disorder.

E. It cannot be established that an organic factor initiated and maintained the disturbance (e.g., repeated intoxication from drugs or alcohol).

DIAGNOSIS OF DEPRESSION
AND OTHER MOOD DISORDERS IN CHILDREN

Mood disturbance in children has been a subject of considerable debate. Some persons maintain that age-specific criteria are important and necessitate a more inferential diagnosis on the part of the clinician, while others feel that a straightforward application of the adult diagnostic criteria is sufficient and valid in childhood. It is crucial for the diagnosis, however, that the mood disturbance be primary and not secondary to some other disorder. In childhood, a number of other disorders, such as Attention-Deficit Hyperactivity Disorder, Conduct Disorders, and developmental disabilities, are known to frequently and regularly produce at least some demoralization. Similarly, when mood disturbance is mild and appears to stem from acute psychosocial stress, a diagnosis of Adjustment Disorder should be considered. If the quality of the mood disturbance is mild but chronic, however, Dysthymia is appropriate. Of the mood disorders, Depressive Disorders have been the most frequently identified within the pediatric age group, but there is growing evidence that Manic Episodes are underdiagnosed in adolescents.

Much attention has been directed toward the diagnosis of depression in children in the past decade. Child psychiatrists generally agree on two facts: (1) that Major Depression is less common in children than in adults, particularly in prepubertal populations; but also (2) that Major Depression has generally been underdiagnosed in children until the last few years (Carlson & Cantwell, 1982b; Kovacs et al., 1984a,b; Rutter et al., 1986).

DSM-III-R carefully spells out the diagnostic criteria for this group of disorders, with few, relatively minor modifications for children. An important change in the criteria for Major Depressive Episode is the specification that irritable mood can be substituted for depressed mood in children and adolescents and is equivalent to diminished interest in activities or ability to concentrate as rated by subjective account or observation by others. This is indicated by research (Carlson & Cantwell, 1982; Kovacs et al., 1984a), but brings up complex differential diagnostic issues since antisocial behavior has a strong association with depression in children and adolescents. However, the differential diagnosis from Oppositional Defiant Disorder is made more difficult by this (probably wise) specification. This change also has major implications for pediatric cases where discrepancies between child and parent reports are common.

Other revisions include the specification, if present, for seasonal pattern for all Mood Disorders. This is relevant for children, as seasonality has been demonstrated in the pediatric age group (e.g., Rosenthal et al., 1986). In addition, the duration criterion for Dysthymia and Cyclothymia has been shortened from two years to one year for children and adolescents. The further specification of early onset (before age 21) for Dysthymia is a useful and even satisfying turn of events. Studies by Mendlewicz and Baron (1981) and others demonstrating a higher rate of Mood Disorders in the relatives of early- compared to late-onset probands has been validated in a number of studies (e.g., Weissman et al., 1986; Klein et al., 1988)—an instance where child-based research has had significant impact on the general classification scheme. Finally, failure to make expected weight gains instead of actual weight loss is the other modification of the criteria for Major Depressive Episode to accommodate childhood/adolescent symptoms.

In general, the DSM-III-R criteria have been maintained across age groups. The rationale for this is that concepts such as "masked" depression or depressive "equivalents" have not been validated and do not seem necessary for current research models (Beardslee et al., 1985).

Several diagnostic patterns specific to childhood should be stressed. In children, the Depressive Disorders have strong associations with both Conduct Disorders and Separation Anxiety Disorder. By contrast, the adolescent group seems to follow a pattern of associated disturbance seen in adult Major Depression (Geller et al., 1985; Puig-Antich, 1986). In prepubertal children, there is equal incidence in males and females for all of the Mood Disorders, while in older groups, females predominate.

Dysthymia is still probably underutilized as a diagnosis in children. Frequently children with Attention-Deficit Hyperactivity Disorder, Conduct Disorders, Mental Retardation, or severe specific developmental disabilities will have associated low self-esteem, tearfulness, and decreased enjoyment of activities. The diagnosis of Dysthymia should be made more frequently in association with these other disorders. Use of multiple diagnoses would avoid the less fruitful either/or debate and an inappropriate use of Major Depression as the sole diagnosis. Moreover, Kovacs and colleagues (Kovacs et al., 1984a,b) have shown that children may alternate between Dysthymia and Major Depression, and that Dysthymia is an important predictor for occurrence of Depressive Disorder, particularly in prepubertal children.

Mania is extremely rare in prepubertal children. Recently, however, there have been excellent studies pointing to the fact that the diagnosis of Mania in adolescents is overlooked by child psychiatrists. This oversight is quite striking, since analyses of patient charts suggest that patients clearly met the typical criteria for Manic Episode as outlined in DSM-III (Carlson & Cantwell, 1982b). Increased awareness and alertness on the part of the clinician diagnosing adolescents may circumvent more severe complications, particularly in view of the possible benefits from lithium treatment, which might not be considered if the diagnosis of Mania is not made.

In conclusion, Mood Disorders have probably been underdiagnosed in children, and research in this area was neglected until very recently. From what is known, it appears that Mania is underdiagnosed in adolescents and Major Depression is underdiagnosed in prepubertal children. In the latter group, males and females have equal incidence, and associated disturbances of Conduct Disorder, Separation Anxiety, or other disorders may be common.

The changes in DSM-III-R are, in general, welcome. They allow a one-year duration for children and adolescents for Cyclothymia and Dysthymia and permit the substitution of irritability for depressed mood. For children as well as adults a number of key symptoms can now be scored if observed by others even without subjective report. A possible effect, however, might be greater difficulty in distinguishing irritability in Oppositional Defiant Disorder from Major Depression since the two disorders are strongly associated. If, for example, a child is inattentive, has low self-esteem, and is irritable, it may be difficult to operationalize the distinction. While Oppositional Defiant Disorder specifies that behaviors should not occur exclusively during a Major Depressive or Dysthymic Episode, in some children this distinction may be problematic.

CASE HISTORIES

Eric

For the past three months, nine-year-old Eric has expressed fearfulness about attending catechism classes after school. In spite of excellent functioning in the studies, he becomes upset at the prospect of spending three hours in the class. He reports a mixture of worries about failure and complains of stomachaches and headaches. Primarily, he feels sad, and for the past few weeks he has been unable to enjoy his usual school activities. Going to sleep is troublesome too, because he is worried about doing poorly in school and he frequently awakens several times during the night. At the same time, his school performance has begun to decline from all As to mostly B grades, because of missing school and difficulty in concentrating. He has become very blue and on several occasions he has burst into tears for no apparent reason.

His mother has had three Major Depressive Episodes. During their 20 years of marriage, the parents have had continuing marital problems. Eric and his two brothers have often been the center of their disputes. Although shy, Eric is a likable child and has always been a good student. In the past, he has attended summer camp, and, though he was somewhat homesick, he seemed to enjoy the activities. He has stayed overnight several times with friends who live nearby, but does appear to be somewhat tied to his mother.

During the interview, Eric suddenly began to sob that he felt terrible all the time and several times said that he would be better off dead, although he denied any specific suicidal plan. He feels guilty that he is such a worry to his parents.

Diagnosis

Axis I:	296.21 Major Depression, Single Episode
	309.21 Separation Anxiety Disorder
Axis II:	V71.09 No diagnosis on Axis II

Axis III: None
Axis IV: Severity: 4—Moderate (predominantly enduring
circumstances)
Stressors: family discord
Axis V: Current GAF: 70
Highest GAF past year: 85

Discussion

Eric presents with symptoms of depression and separation anxiety. He meets criteria for Major Depression, Single Episode, while anxiety symptoms do not have sufficient severity or chronicity for the diagnosis of Separation Anxiety Disorder. Although his depressive symptoms are mild, duration of less than one year rules out a diagnosis of Dysthymia, Early Onset. Here, too, the British Axis V choices of Discordant Intrafamilial Relationships or Mental Disturbance in Other Family Members would be more informative clinically, although these stressors can be indicated in addition to the rating.

Samuel

Samuel was an 11-year-old black child referred to the child psychiatry clinic for attempted suicide. He had concocted a mixture of medicines prescribed to his mother—antibiotics, sleeping pills, and aspirins—and consumed it in an attempt to kill himself. He slept at home for almost two days; when he was finally awakened by his mother, she brought him to the hospital.

Samuel lives in an inner-city neighborhood and since second grade has been in trouble repeatedly for stealing and breaking into empty houses. In school he has had academic difficulties and is assigned to a reading disability classroom for part of each day.

The mother is known to abuse alcohol and may also have been a prostitute. She has had several Major Depressive Episodes but has never been treated. Samuel's father has not been in contact with her since Samuel was born.

During the interview Samuel appeared sad and cried at one point, his thin shoulders shaking. He reported having severe blue periods which had been continuous for the past month. During these periods he thinks that he might be better off dead. Recently, he has started to wake up in the middle of the night. He also indicated that of late he had been avoiding his usual neighborhood "gang."

Diagnosis

Axis I:	296.23 Major Depression, Single Episode
	312.20 Conduct Disorder (Group Type)
Axis II:	315.00 Developmental Reading Disorder
Axis III:	None
Axis IV:	Severity: 5 — Severe (predominantly enduring circumstances)
	Stressor(s): inconsistent parenting; academic difficulties
Axis V:	Current GAF: 45
	Highest GAF past year: 50

Discussion

Samuel's symptoms are of a severe Major Depressive Episode that has lasted for several weeks. This seems to be the first occurrence but there may be a possibility of an underlying depression, existing for many years. If this is the case, a provisional diagnosis of Dysthymia should also be considered. This case reflects the puzzling fact that, during childhood, Major Depression is commonly found in males who have a diagnosis of Conduct Disorder. In addition, there is the association between Conduct Disorder and Developmental Reading Disorder, which has been demonstrated so effectively by British epidemiological studies (Rutter et al., 1970). Here, too, British Axis V coding would indicate the associated abnormal psychosocial situations and would be more informative. It is strongly recommended that the stressors be recorded in addition to the Axis IV rating for future reference.

Chapter 12

Disruptive Behavior Disorders

A useful change in DSM-III-R is that Attention-Deficit Hyperactivity Disorder, Oppositional Defiant Disorder, and Conduct Disorders are brought together under a new heading: Disruptive Behavior Disorders. Because the three disorders are heavily associated with each other and are defined by somewhat similar behaviors, considerable attention went into the reshaping of this section. Even with the newer, more careful delineation between these syndromes, however, the relationship among them remains complex. For example, a large prospective follow-up of hyperactive boys found both initial and continuing hyperactivity to predict the later development of Conduct Disorder and Antisocial Personality Disorder (Gittelman et al., 1985).

DISRUPTIVE BEHAVIOR DISORDERS

Summary of DSM-III-R Changes
Rather extensive empirical work has been carried out on the associated features and differential diagnosis between Attention-Deficit Hyperactivity Disorder and Conduct Disorder (Taylor, 1988). The major changes, all improvements over DSM-III, are that hyperactivity is back in the title of Attention-Deficit Disorder (now called Attention-Deficit Hyperactivity Disorder) and the DSM-III category of Attention-Deficit Disorder With-

TABLE 24
Disruptive Behavior Disorders: DSM-III-R Axis I Codes

314.01	Attention-Deficit Hyperactivity Disorder
	Conduct Disorder
312.20	Group Type
312.00	Solitary Aggressive Type
312.90	Undifferentiated Type
313.81	Oppositional Defiant Disorder

(Under Other Disorders of Infancy, Childhood, and Adolescence)
314.00   Undifferentiated Attention-Deficit Disorder

out Hyperactivity has been eliminated. These decisions were based on several studies demonstrating that hyperactivity is a crucial part of the disorder (Taylor, 1988; Gittelman et al., 1985) and that attention is difficult to operationalize in a way that would resolve diagnostic dilemmas. The decision to drop Attention-Deficit Disorder Without Hyperactivity remains controversial. In favor of its removal was the fact that it was seldom used, and some evidence suggests that it was an even more heterogeneous group than Attention-Deficit Disorder with Hyperactivity (e.g., Lahey et al. 1984). The residual category of Undifferentiated Attention-Deficit Disorder is now placed in the "Other Disorders of Infancy, Childhood, or Adolescence" section.

Oppositional Disorder was renamed Oppositional Defiant Disorder to highlight the fact that the threshold for diagnosis has been raised, and that the distinctive behaviors are more likely to be a precursor of Conduct Disorder.

Conduct Disorder has somewhat more severe and specific criteria for diagnosis in DSM-III-R, but the most striking change is the decreased number of subcategories. Now the choice is between Group Type, Solitary Aggressive Type, and Undifferentiated. It is anticipated that the Undifferentiated subcategory will be heavily used because so many children will fall between the first two definitions (see case example at the end of this chapter).

ATTENTION-DEFICIT HYPERACTIVITY DISORDER
Within this category the emphasis is now equally divided between hyperactivity, attentional problems, and impulsivity. Poor impulse control is

closely associated with both attention problems and excessive motor restlessness, and DSM-III-R avoids the problematic categorization of these problem behaviors. Hyperactivity per se tends to diminish in adolescence. The course of the disorder typically follows one of three patterns: (1) All symptoms continue into adulthood with possible development of Antisocial Personality Disorder; (2) symptoms dissipate or disappear in adolescence; or (3) hyperactivity disappears but inattention, impulsivity, and social immaturity persist into adolescence and adulthood. There have not been enough coded follow-up studies to record frequency patterns.

A child displaying these types of difficulties usually comes to the attention of professionals during the early school years, but parents often report onset by age three. In school, difficulties increase in completing work and following or listening to directions because the situation demands sustained attention in a group setting where distracting stimuli are always present. Symptoms vary with time and place, home versus school. Tasks requiring "self-application" are more likely to exacerbate symptoms than one-to-one relationships or new situations. The variability of the symptoms may require using multiple informants to obtain an overview of the problem. Primary consideration should be given to the reports of teachers, however, because their views may be considerably more objective than those of the parents.

Eight of 14 symptoms are currently required by the DSM-III-R criteria, with a duration period of at least six months. Age of onset is set at before age seven though in almost half of the cases onset is reported before age four. The problems are not usually recognized however, until after the child has entered school. In addition, severity codes of Mild, Moderate, or Severe are required. Some difference in symptoms is noticeable between different age groups, with younger children displaying more motor overactivity, and older children generally exhibiting excessive fidgeting, restlessness, or impulsive behaviors. Inattention and distractibility are evident in failure to complete assignments or follow instructions, or by careless performance of tasks. The criteria are specifically stated to be aimed at the eight-to-10-year-old age group. If the child is younger, more symptoms would be expected; if older, less would be apparent.

Coding

Axis II. If Attention-Deficit Hyperactivity Disorder is coded as an Axis I disorder, one is often likely to encounter Axis II disorders within the category of Specific Developmental Disorders. These should be carefully

TABLE 25
314.01 Attention-Deficit Hyperactivity Disorder: Diagnostic Criteria

Note: Consider a criterion met only if the behavior is considerably more frequent than that of most people of the same mental age.

A. A disturbance of at least six months during which at least eight of the following are present:
    1. Often fidgets with hands or feet or squirms in seat (in adolescents, may be limited to subjective feelings of restlessness)
    2. Has difficulty remaining seated when required to do so
    3. Is easily distracted by extraneous stimuli
    4. Has difficulty awaiting turn in games or group situations
    5. Often blurts out answers to questions before they have been completed
    6. Has difficulty following through on instructions from others (not due to oppositional behavior or failure of comprehension) (e.g., fails to finish chores)
    7. Has difficulty sustaining attention in tasks or play activities
    8. Often shifts from one uncompleted activity to another
    9. Has difficulty playing quietly
    10. Often talks excessively
    11. Often interrupts or intrudes on others (e.g., butts into other children's games)
    12. Often does not seem to listen to what is being said to him or her
    13. Often loses things necessary for tasks or activities at school or at home (e.g., toys, pencils, books, assignments)
    14. Often engages in physically dangerous activities without considering possible consequences (not for the purpose of thrill seeking) (e.g., runs into street without looking)

Note: The above items are listed in descending order of discriminating power based on data from a national field trial of the DSM-III-R criteria for Disruptive Behavior Disorders.

B. Onset before the age of seven.

C. Does not meet the criteria for a Pervasive Developmental Disorder.

Criteria for severity of Attention-Deficit Hyperactivity Disorder
Mild: Few, if any, symptoms in excess of those required to make the diagnosis and only minimal or no impairment in school and social functioning.
Moderate: Symptoms or functional impairment intermediate between "Mild" and "Severe."
Severe: Many symptoms in excess of those required to make the diagnosis *and* significant and pervasive impairment in functioning at home and school and with peers.

coded because of the association between impaired attention and hyperactivity with other developmental deficiencies.

Although DSM-III-R does not suggest a more limiting IQ cutoff, association with mild to moderate intellectual impairment is well documented, and in such cases Mild to Moderate Mental Retardation should be coded on Axis II. For research purposes, many centers are defining their own IQ limits in order to eliminate cases where factors contributing to the symptom pattern may be contaminated or largely determined by low intelligence.

Axis III. Diagnosed neurological disorders should be included on Axis III, along with any other physical illness. In some research settings, a case with a known neurological impairment may be excluded as a means of protecting a "pure" classification of the syndrome under research. This occurs in only about 5% of the cases. "Soft" signs, however, are more commonly noted, as well as motor/perceptual dysfunctions (coded now on Axis II—see 315.40).

Axis IV. Psychosocial stressors. These should always be rated and the specific stressor noted, especially since the appearance of the same disorder within family groupings is more common than in the general population, and there is an association with adult substance abuse and antisocial behaviors among family members (Stewart et al., 1980). Studies focusing on heritable and social factors are needed to help delineate the etiology of the syndrome more clearly.

Axis V. Adaptive functioning. This is also important, as a child with Attention-Deficit Hyperactivity Disorder frequently encounters academic difficulties which have implications for his or her future, as well as a possible effect on the course of the illness. It is also common for these children to experience problems in social functioning. Consideration given to this aspect of diagnosis will influence treatment interventions for social and academic problems, and outcome at follow-up may be best predicted by this measure.

Diagnostic Issues and Differential Diagnoses

The absence of subtypes in DSM-III-R should not mislead anyone into thinking that Attention-Deficit Hyperactivity Disorder is now a singular, homogeneous disorder. Careful scrutiny of the 14 behavioral items that define the syndrome shows that selection of primarily inattentive or restless behaviors will still meet the criteria, thus allowing for some equivalent of Attention-Deficit Disorder Without Hyperactivity to be diagnosed.

Only Pervasive Developmental Disorder on Axis II preempts the diagnosis of Attention-Deficit Hyperactivity Disorder. It is possible to make an additional diagnosis of Attention-Deficit Hyperactivity Disorder with Mood Disorders or with Schizophrenia. In such cases, however, one should be convinced that the hyperactivity and inattention do not stem from the other disorders.

The most difficult aspect of the Attention-Deficit Hyperactivity Disorder diagnosis is in assessing the extent and severity of inappropriate behaviors. DSM-III-R states that the disorder is usually manifest in most situations, but to varying degrees. Empirical data support the somewhat greater validity of school observations over those in other settings due to the greater uniformity of classroom situations and the presence of attention-demanding tasks (Rapoport & Benoit, 1975).

Certain conditions may cause similar behaviors that should be distinguished from Attention-Deficit Hyperactivity Disorder. Age-appropriate overactivity is distinguished by the quality of the activity. By nature it would not be haphazard or disorganized. An inadequate, disorganized, chaotic environment might cause a child to simulate such behavior. The clinician must try to objectively evaluate all the circumstances surrounding the child. Specific learning disabilities may produce classroom restlessness, as can Mild to Moderate Mental Retardation, or classroom placement mismatched to ability level. Other possibilities to eliminate are acute situational reactions or Adjustment Disorder. In these cases Axis IV and V should be helpful. Autistic Disorder precludes the use of this diagnosis. In the case of Mental Retardation, only Mild or Moderate diagnoses should be double coded. Profound or Severe Mental Retardation should preempt an Attention-Deficit Hyperactivity Disorder diagnosis. Conduct Disorder and Oppositional Defiant Disorder may also be separately coded along with Attention-Deficit Hyperactivity Disorder on Axis I, but one would not use both Conduct Disorder and Oppositional Defiant Disorder together.

CONDUCT DISORDER

The DSM-III category of Conduct Disorder raised a lot of controversy concerning the validity of its subtypes, especially for application to prepubertal cases. In DSM-III-R, Conduct Disorder is defined in much the same way, but the criteria are more clear and somewhat more applicable for females than were those in DSM-III. The new subgroups—"Group Type," "Solitary Aggressive Type," and "Undifferentiated"—will undoubtedly also be controversial. It may well be that "Undifferentiated" will be the most popular (see case history of Reginald at the end of this chapter). However, the previous subtyping was unworkable (e.g., in a study by Prendergast et al. [1988], trained research teams could only agree on subtypes in nine of 23 cases considered to have Conduct Disorder). In the absence of new empirical data, fewer subcategories seems preferable to more. Despite the subtypes issue, the nature of conduct disordered behaviors seems to be persistent and repetitive, their consequences being more serious than a mischievous prank. Mild forms tend to dissipate with maturity, but more severe forms are likely to be chronic.

Other Axis I disorders often associated with Conduct Disorder are Attention-Deficit Hyperactivity Disorder and Substance Use Disorder. For patients over age 18, a diagnosis of Antisocial Personality Disorder will also be made. On Axis II, Specific Developmental Disorders and Mental Retardation are commonly found in conjunction with this category of illness. Social stressors on Axis IV often center on difficulties in the home or a family history of alcohol dependence. Often economic factors, size of the family, and inconsistent or poor parenting are predisposing factors. On Axis V coding should evaluate academic and social functioning, as these are often areas of impairment.

Duration greater than a few months eliminates the question of diagnosing an Adjustment Disorder. Isolated instances of antisocial conduct, V Code 71.02 (Childhood or Adolescent Antisocial Behavior), are relatively easy to distinguish from Conduct Disorders because they are usually limited in occurrence and do not show the lack of academic achievement and poor social relations that characterize the conduct-disordered child. It is uncertain whether onset of Intermittent Explosive Disorder (312.34) begins in childhood, but this diagnosis should also be considered for the postpubertal child who does not meet criteria for Conduct Disorder.

With Oppositional Defiant Disorder, similar characteristics of attitude may prevail, but without evidence of violation of the basic rights of others or major rules and social norms. Virtually all cases diagnosed as Conduct Disorder will meet the criteria for Oppositional Defiant Disorder; however, only the former diagnosis would be made.

An Axis I diagnosis of Attention-Deficit Hyperactivity Disorder or Major Depression would also be coded. If a Specific Developmental Disorder or Mental Retardation is also present, it should also be coded on Axis II.

TABLE 26
Conduct Disorder: Diagnostic Criteria

A.   A disturbance of conduct lasting at least six months, during which at least three of the following have been present:
  1.   Has stolen without confrontation of a victim on more than one occasion (including forgery)
  2.   Has run away from home overnight at least twice while living in parental or parental surrogate home (or once without returning)
  3.   Often lies (other than to avoid physical or sexual abuse)
  4.   Has deliberately engaged in fire setting
  5.   Is often truant from school (for older person, absent from work)
  6.   Has broken into someone else's house, building, or car
  7.   Has deliberately destroyed others' property (other than by fire setting)
  8.   Has been physically cruel to animals
  9.   Has forced someone into sexual activity with him or her
  10.   Has used a weapon in more than one fight
  11.   Often initiates physical fights
  12.   Has stolen with confrontation of a victim (e.g., mugging, purse snatching, extortion, armed robbery)
  13.   Has been physically cruel to people

Note: The above items are listed in descending order of discriminating power based on data from a national field trial of the DSM-III-R criteria for Disruptive Behavior Disorders.

B.   If 18 or older, does not meet criteria for Antisocial Personality Disorder.

Criteria for severity of Conduct Disorder:
Mild: Few if any conduct problems in excess of those required to make the diagnosis and conduct problems cause only minor harm to others.
Moderate: Number of conduct problems and effect on others intermediate between "Mild" and "Severe."
Severe: Many conduct problems in excess of those required to make the diagnosis or conduct problems cause considerable harm to others (e.g., serious physical injury to victims, extensive vandalism or theft, prolonged absence from home).

OPPOSITIONAL DEFIANT DISORDER

This diagnosis should not be used for children aged 18 to 36 months when similar behaviors are considered normal. Conduct Disorder, as mentioned before, is characterized by more serious violation of others' rights and societal norms, although Oppositional Defiant Disorder in many instances

TABLE 27
Conduct Disorder Subtypes: Essential Features

a. Group Type: Predominate problems occur mainly as group activity with peers. Aggressive physical behavior may or may not be present.

b. Solitary Aggressive Type: Predominance of aggressive physical behavior, usually toward both adults and peers, initiated by the person (not as a group activity).

c. Undifferentiated Type: For children or adolescents with Conduct Disorder with a mixture of clinical features that cannot be classified as either Solitary Aggressive Type or Group Type.

is a precursor of Conduct Disorder. Differentiation from childhood onset of Dysthymic Disorder or Major Depression may be difficult (see Chapter 11), as irritability may now be coded instead of depressed mood for childhood cases of Major Depression. Instances of Attention-Deficit Hyperactivity Disorder and mild to moderate forms of Mental Retardation are associated conditions and should be coded on the appropriate axis. Attention-Deficit Hyperactivity Disorder has a similar symptom picture: obstinacy, stubbornness, negativism, temper outbursts, lack of response to discipline, and so forth. However, if the quality of these characteristics is more striking than in similar Attention-Deficit Hyperactivity Disorder cases, an additional diagnosis of Oppositional Defiant Disorder would be given. If the subject is over the age of 18 and does not meet criteria for Passive-Aggressive Personality Disorder, Oppositional Defiant Disorder should be considered.

A controversial issue concerning this diagnosis is one of degree, as it seems difficult to differentiate when the occurrence of these symptoms is normal, especially when viewing typical adolescent emancipation behaviors or temper outbursts in young children. Many felt the DSM-III Oppositional Disorder to be a heterogeneous group better served by other diagnoses (e.g., Rey et al., 1988). DSM-III-R has partially addressed this controversy by raising the threshold considerably for this diagnosis. Conscientious coding of this category, along with other applicable Axis I and II disorders, will help to determine the usefulness or validity of this category as a disorder.

TABLE 28
313.81 Oppositional Defiant Disorder: Diagnostic Criteria

Note: Consider a criterion met only if the behavior is considerably more frequent than that of most people of the same mental age.

A. A disturbance of at least six months during which at least five of the following are present:
    1. Often loses temper
    2. Often argues with adults
    3. Often actively defies or refuses adult requests or rules (e.g., refuses to do chores at home)
    4. Often deliberately does things that annoy other people (e.g., grabs other children's hats)
    5. Often blames others for his or her own mistakes
    6. Is often touchy or easily annoyed by others
    7. Is often angry and resentful
    8. Is often spiteful or vindictive
    9. Often swears or uses obscene language

Note: The above items are listed in descending order of discriminating power based on data from a national field trial of the DSM-III-R criteria for Disruptive Behavior Disorders.

B. Does not meet the criteria for Conduct Disorder, and does not occur exclusively during the course of a psychotic disorder, Dysthymia, or a Major Depressive, Hypomanic, or Manic Episode.

Criteria for severity of Oppositional Defiant Disorder:
Mild: Few, if any, symptoms in excess of those required to make the diagnosis *and* only minimal or no impairment in school and social functioning.
Moderate: Symptoms or functional impairment intermediate between "Mild" and "Severe."
Severe: Many symptoms in excess of those required to make the diagnosis *and* significant and pervasive impairment in functioning at home and school and with other adults and peers.

SUMMARY OF DIAGNOSTIC ISSUES:
DISRUPTIVE BEHAVIOR DISORDERS

The Disruptive Behavior Disorders section of DSM-III-R shows clear superiority over the handling of these three disorders in DSM-III, but major concerns remain. On the positive side is the greater ease of differentiating both Oppositional Defiant Disorder and Attention-Deficit Hyperactivity Disorder from normal behavior. Defining characteristics are more severe, more specific, and, in the case of Attention-Deficit Hyperactivity Disorder, make specific reference to a comparison with peers and to disturbance across situations. Placing the three disorders within a separate category highlights their complex interrelationships as well as the complexity of differential diagnosis.

Controversy remains, however, over several other changes. The decision to eliminate Attention-Deficit Disorder Without Hyperactivity has been criticized on the grounds that although the category did appear heterogeneous, the relatively few empirical data available made the decision premature. The last-minute inclusion under "Other Disorders of Infancy, Childhood, or Adolescence" of Undifferentiated Attention-Deficit Disorder (314.00) represents waffling on this issue. Everyone applauds the increased threshold for the diagnosis of Oppositional Defiant Disorder, but some would say it has not gone far enough and that it will still be applied in relatively trivial situations.

Perhaps most controversial was the change to the Conduct Disorder subtypes. This is a problematic issue, as both interrater reliability and predictive validity were not satisfactorily demonstrated for the old types, while preliminary opinion suggests that too many children will slip through the newer, albeit simpler subgroups and most will end up as Undifferentiated Type (Rutter, 1988). There is extremely important research to be done in order to predict follow-up status for this very high-risk group, an area of vital concern for future work on classification in child psychiatry.

CASE HISTORIES

Regina
Six-year-old Regina was brought to the clinic by her parents, who stated that the child was ruining their marriage. The father feels that the mother spoils the girl with inconsistent discipline and the mother feels that she tries her best without success.

For at least the past three years, Regina has been "extremely difficult." She is willful and the "terrible twos" were never outgrown. Regina often spoils family treats planned for her by misbehaving and having friends sent home. At the private co-op school she attends, the teachers often have her play quietly by herself because she irritates the other children. In turn, the other children respond to her, and she often ends up throwing things or slapping. She lisps and talks baby talk, but this has improved somewhat in the past year. Developmental milestones have been normal. She is considered quite bright in school. At the clinic interview, Regina enjoyed the individual attention shown her but was demanding in structuring the examination and tried to keep the playroom toys even though she was told that she couldn't. She refused to help clean up at the end of the session, saying she didn't feel like it.

Both parents are invested in the child but find her violent temper tantrums hard to handle.

Diagnosis

Axis I: 313.81 Oppositional Defiant Disorder (Mild)
Axis II: 315.39 Developmental Articulation Disorder
Axis III: None
Axis IV: Severity: 1—None
            Stressor(s): N/A
Axis V: Current GAF: 65
            Highest GAF past year: 60

Discussion

Regina is considered to have Oppositional Defiant Disorder. She does not meet criteria for Attention-Deficit Hyperactivity Disorder or Conduct Disorder, possibly because of her relatively young age. It will be of considerable interest to see the eventual outcome for this girl, as the behaviors resemble some of those of Passive-Aggressive Personality Disorder. Other studies suggest that Dysthymia Disorder or Major Depression is a likely outcome. The parents are eager for counseling and it is hoped behavior therapy will be helpful in shaping some positive behaviors. It is of interest that Regina has a Mild Developmental Articulation Disorder which is often associated with behavioral disturbance.

Reginald

Reginald, an 11-year-old black child, was brought to the clinic by his mother (at the request of his school) because of continued fighting and bullying. His mother claims that Reginald has always been a "handful," but now feels that he gets out of line too often and that she can no longer control him. She recently found numerous items in his room that she believes to be stolen, and she has received several reports from neighbors about minor property damage. He lies constantly, even if caught and confronted. She attributes part of the problem to the influence of two older neighborhood boys with whom Reginald spends a lot of time. He was recently suspended from school along with these two friends for having set up a blockade to catch younger kids on the way home from school. The youths made small demands for money, but Reginald claimed that they intended no harm. There was, however, an incident in which a younger girl fell (or was pushed) off her bike.

Reginald has repeated both first and second grades. His teachers report that he is easily frustrated, is failing most subjects, and is constantly out of his seat creating a disruption. He usually looks unhappy and upset. This kind of behavior is viewed as attention seeking. He works much better in the small resource class to which he is assigned two hours a day for help in reading. Most of the rest of his day is spent in the principal's office.

Reginald is the second oldest of four children in a one-parent home. His natural father left the home over a year ago, and the mother works two part-time jobs to make ends meet. This means that the children are left unsupervised a good part of the day, with Reginald's 15-year-old sister taking most of the responsibility. Reginald does not get along with this sister; he will hit and bite her if she tries to manage him.

On interview, Reginald spoke little and looked miserable. When asked, he denied feeling "blue" but complained that his sister was "mean" to him. The clinic evaluation testing showed that Verbal IQ=57, Performance IQ=78, and Full Scale IQ=66.

Diagnosis
    Axis I: 312.90 Conduct Disorder, Undifferentiated Type
                (Moderate)
    Axis II: 317.00 Mild Mental Retardation
    Axis IV: Severity: 4—Moderate (Predominantly enduring
                circumstances)
                Stressor(s): Family factors
    Axis V: Current GAF: 35
                Highest GAF past year: 40

Discussion
Reginald meets the general DSM-III-R criteria for Conduct Disorder since the problems highlighted include a continued pattern lasting over six months that includes at least three antisocial behaviors: stealing, vandalism, and extortion. Since his behaviors involve aggressive deeds and it is difficult to determine subtype based on solitary or group behavior, the mixed features indicate Undifferentiated Type.

In addition, Reginald has a mild form of Mental Retardation. His IQ testing indicates that his school placement is probably inadequate. Reginald may also have specific developmental difficulties, but the present data do not allow us to make this assessment. It is not clear whether his level of academic backwardness is beyond that predicted by the behavioral disturbance together with the Mild Mental Retardation. Reginald's depressed demeanor is a common attribute in conduct-disordered children at odds with their caretakers and does not merit an additional coding for a Mood Disorder.

Stuart

Eight-year-old Stuart was referred to the local child guidance clinic by his physician because of a history of overactivity, school problems, onset of illness within the family, and poor social relations.

The mother reported that Stuart was overly active as an infant and toddler. His teachers found him difficult to control once he started school. He is described as extremely impulsive and distractible, moving about tirelessly from one activity to the next. At present he knows the alphabet and a few words on sight, but he cannot read a full sentence. His math skills are also minimal. Because of these learning difficulties, Stuart is in a small, self-contained class for learning-disabled children. His teacher reports that he is immature and restless, responds best in a structured, one-on-one situation, but is considered the class pest because he is continually annoying the other children and is disobedient.

Since the start of the school year, he has soiled his pants on numerous occasions, does not seem to have any special friends, and has been reported on different occasions by the school bus driver for hitting other children and throwing things on the bus.

His mother reports that Stuart responds to some disciplining, but lately he has started sassing back and swearing at her. He frequently throws temper tantrums, especially if she asks him to do something or denies his requests. His constant badgering and whining are irritating for her, especially since her husband has been in and out of the hospital for the past six months with a terminal illness. Because of his illness, the father has been minimally involved with Stuart's discipline for the last two years.

Diagnosis

Axis I: 314.01 Attention-Deficit Hyperactivity Disorder (Moderate)
313.81 Oppositional Defiant Disorder (Mild)
307.70 Functional Encopresis

Axis II: 315.00 Developmental Reading Disorder
315.10 Developmental Arithmetic Disorder
Axis IV: Severity: 5 — Severe (Predominantly enduring
circumstances)
Stressor(s): Learning difficulties, illness in parent
Axis V: Current: 45
Past year: 50

Discussion
Stuart has symptoms typical of Attention-Deficit Hyperactivity Disorder, as well as the additional burden of learning problems. His oppositional behavior (disobedience, throwing, hitting, tantrums) and soiling seem to coincide with the worsening of his father's illness. Because these behaviors have persisted for so long, diagnoses of Oppositional Defiant Disorder and Functional Encopresis are made. The stressor is recorded on Axis IV rather than using an Adjustment Disorder diagnosis.

Chapter 13

Anxiety Disorders

The dysfunctions within the specific section of Anxiety Disorders of Childhood or Adolescence are considered to be specific to that particular age group. These are Separation Anxiety Disorder, Avoidant Disorder of Childhood or Adolescence, and Overanxious Disorder. Other DSM-III-R Anxiety Disorders that occur regularly in children and adolescents include Phobic Disorders, Post-traumatic Stress Disorder, and Obsessive Compulsive Disorder. The experience of anxiety and its resultant effects is the major symptomatic component of this group of disorders.

The acute anxiety state is experienced as an overwhelming sense of fear and dread that generally incapacitates the individual for a period of time. It may also induce physiological responses. Often it is initiated in response to certain stimuli or circumstances, as in the case of phobias. Generalized anxiety is a more pervasive attitude of apprehension that keeps the individual in a constant state of vigilance. It is accompanied by signs of tension and autonomic arousal. In children, however, the diagnosis is more difficult since partial syndromes and overlapping subtypes may occur more commonly among clinic patients. This does not seem to be true for adult series of Anxiety Disorders.

ANXIETY DISORDERS OF CHILDHOOD OR ADOLESCENCE

Fear of separation, social avoidance, and persistent worry are the major elements of the anxiety manifest within these disorders. Diagnosis of these disorders should be made when the manifest anxiety is the most salient

TABLE 29
Anxiety Disorders of Childhood or Adolescence: DSM-III-R Axis I Codes

309.21	Separation Anxiety Disorder
313.21	Avoidant Disorder of Childhood or Adolescence
313.00	Overanxious Disorder

feature, rather than being attributable to any other major disorder. In some cases where criteria for another disorder are met, there may be double coding, as discussed below; however, these categories would never be used in conjunction with Pervasive Developmental Disorder, Schizophrenia, or other psychotic disorders since anxiety displayed under those conditions is considered to be part of the syndrome.

Note that Anxiety Disorders are strongly inter-associated and often more than one of the disorders discussed in this section will be coded (see Last et al., 1987). Similarly, as in adults, Depression is strongly associated (Kolvin et al., 1984). For all the Anxiety Disorders, DSM-III-R has eliminated the diagnostic hierarchy under which another diagnosis such as Major Depression preempts the diagnosis of an Anxiety Disorder. One still must make the distinction whether the anxiety occurs *only* in relation to, or is a symptom of, a mood episode. The elimination of this rule is welcome as the complex relationship will not be untangled if prejudgments confound diagnostic decisions.

Separation Anxiety Disorder
In Separation Anxiety Disorder, as the name suggests, anxiety is aroused upon separation from familiar persons, usually the parents, or upon leaving the home and entering new territory. The reaction is excessive and anticipated separation may induce somatic complaints or symptoms. After separation has occurred, the child may be inconsolable and express fears that the parent may not return or that some tragedy will ensue that will prevent the child from ever seeing the parent again.

Onset of this type of symptom pattern is often reported during the preschool years, but distinction must be made from a normal degree of separation anxiety that ensues at this age. The most extreme form of the disorder is reported to occur in prepubertal children, who may refuse to go to school in order to avoid the trauma of separation. True school phobia entails a fear of the actual school setting and persists even if accompanied by the parent. Most instances of Separation Anxiety Disorder seem to

TABLE 30
309.21 Separation Anxiety Disorder: Diagnostic Criteria

A. Excessive anxiety concerning separation from those to whom the child is attached, as evidenced by at least three of the following:
  1. Unrealistic and persistent worry about possible harm befalling major attachment figures or fear that they will leave and not return
  2. Unrealistic and persistent worry that an untoward calamitous event will separate the child from a major attachment figure (e.g., the child will be lost, kidnapped, killed, or be the victim of an accident)
  3. Persistent reluctance or refusal to go to school in order to stay with major attachment figures or at home
  4. Persistent reluctance or refusal to go to sleep without being near a major attachment figure or to go to sleep away from home
  5. Persistent avoidance of being alone, including "clinging" to and "shadowing" major attachment figures
  6. Repeated nightmares involving the theme of separation
  7. Complaints of physical symptoms (e.g., headaches, stomachaches, nausea, or vomiting) on many school days or on other occasions when anticipating separation from major attachment figures
  8. Recurrent signs or complaints of excessive distress in anticipation of separation from home or major attachment figures (e.g., temper tantrums or crying, pleading with parents not to leave)
  9. Recurrent signs of complaints of excessive distress when separated from home or major attachment figures (e.g., wants to return home, needs to call parents when they are absent or when child is away from home)
B. Duration of disturbance of at least two weeks.
C. Onset before the age of 18.
D. Occurrence not exclusively during the course of a Pervasive Developmental Disorder, Schizophrenia, or any other psychotic disorder.

develop in reaction to a major life stress (which should be noted on Axis IV) and follow a variable course of intensity for several years. An unexplained but common denominator in many of these cases is a close-knit, caring family constellation.

The criteria spell out nine different ways anxiety may be evidenced in this disorder and specify that three of these symptoms must be present for a duration of two weeks. If the person is past age 18, this diagnosis is given only when the conditions for Panic Disorder with Agoraphobia are *not* met. Although Separation Anxiety Disorder constitutes a type of phobic reaction, DSM-III-R treats it as a specific disorder of childhood and places it under the childhood disorders. Separation Anxiety and Overanxious

Disorder are strongly associated; a recent clinic-based study by Last et al. (1987), for example, found that one-third of children receiving an Anxiety Disorder diagnosis met criteria for both Separation Anxiety Disorder and Overanxious Disorder.

Avoidant Disorder of Childhood or Adolescence

This disorder is typified by a fear of strangers that predominates to such a degree that social functioning is impaired in an individual who otherwise displays appropriate and affectionate relationships with family members and friends. Age-appropriate social interaction with peers is avoided; however, the degree of individual functional impairment is mild and may result only in feelings of loneliness or mild depression. The required duration is at least six months and age at onset must be greater than two and a half, since stranger anxiety is considered developmentally normal prior to that age. It is typical for onset to occur after starting school where there is an increased demand for social contacts. At any age, this diagnosis is used only if the individual fails to meet the criteria for Avoidant Personality Disorder; later in adolescence, the behavior may be so chronic and pervasive as to favor this diagnosis. The course of the illness may show spontaneous improvement, appear in episodic sequences, or develop into a chronic pattern, though little information has been documented. Children with this disorder are generally unassertive and lack self-confidence. The disorder is often accompanied by other anxiety disorders such as Overanxious Disorder.

Differential diagnosis should take into account the shy, timid child who shows social reticence upon initial encounter but eventually warms up and is able to engage in age-appropriate peer interactions, in contrast to a child incapacitated by extreme impairment in social functioning. A child with Separation Anxiety Disorder fears the separation more than the situation; in Overanxious Disorder, however, the anxiety is not limited to contact with strangers. A diagnosis of Avoidant Personality Disorder is appropriate if the pattern of impaired social relations has persisted for a long period of time and is expressed in virtually all aspects of the subject's life. Adjustment Disorder with Withdrawal involves a recent social stressor and the individual does not exhibit a historical pattern of impaired relationships. The discomfort displayed in Avoidant Disorder of Childhood or Adolescence does not exclude the desire for friendship and affection, whereas in Schizoid Personality Disorder a preference for social isolation is clearly indicated.

Overanxious Disorder

A child with this complaint exhibits anticipatory anxiety which is generalized to include most events requiring some form of judgment or appraisal of the child's performance or appearance. The child's behavior is likely to be characterized by restlessness, nervous habits, perfectionistic tendencies, and need for reinforcement and approval. Onset may be sudden or gradual and will tend to be exacerbated during periods of stress. If the condition persists into adulthood, it may meet the conditions for Generalized Anxiety Disorder or Social Phobia. Occurrence is common in higher socioeconomic levels where performance expectations are high.

The criteria itemize persistent worries and specify that four be present for a period of six months in order to qualify for the diagnosis. The disturbance should not be diagnosed if symptoms can be entirely explained by the concerns of Separation Anxiety Disorder, Avoidant Disorder of Childhood or Adolescence, a Phobic Disorder, or Obsessive Compulsive Disorder, Mood Disorder, Schizophrenia, or Pervasive Developmental

TABLE 31
313.00 Overanxious Disorder: Diagnostic Criteria

A. Excessive or unrealistic anxiety or worry, for a period of six months or longer, as indicated by the frequent occurrence of at least four of the following:
   1. Excessive or unrealistic worry about future events
   2. Excessive or unrealistic concern about the appropriateness of past behavior
   3. Excessive or unrealistic concern about competence in one or more areas (e.g., athletic, academic, social)
   4. Somatic complaints, such as headaches or stomachaches, for which no physical basis can be established
   5. Marked self-consciousness
   6. Excessive need for reassurance about a variety of concerns
   7. Marked feelings of tension or inability to relax
B. If another Axis I disorder is present (e.g., Separation Anxiety Disorder, Phobic Disorder, Obsessive Compulsive Disorder), the focus of the symptoms in A is not limited to it. For example, if Separation Anxiety Disorder is present, the symptoms in A are not exclusively related to anxiety about separation. In addition, the disturbance does not occur only during the course of a psychotic disorder or a Mood Disorder.
C. If 18 or older, does not meet the criteria for Generalized Anxiety Disorder.
D. Occurrence not exclusively during the course of a Pervasive Developmental Disorder, Schizophrenia, or any other psychotic disorder.

Disorder. If Attention-Deficit Hyperactivity Disorder is also evident, both diagnoses should be noted.

Summary of DSM-III-R Changes

DSM-III-R's addition of a group of Anxiety Disorders specifically defined for use with pediatric subjects was welcome for a number of reasons. First, it specifies the frequency with which these disorders occur in childhood, for example, Separation Anxiety Disorder, and spells out in detail the symptoms appropriate at early ages. The definition of Overanxious Disorder is still problematic. Presumably the new criteria facilitate the diagnosis in children when anxiety is present that is inappropriate for the child's developmental level, and with more age-adjusted symptom examples. However, it is not clear how to differentiate Overanxious Disorder from Generalized Anxiety Disorder (see next section) which can, at least in theory, be diagnosed under age 18. In the face of this ambiguity, it is suggested that Generalized Anxiety Disorder be used for all patients aged 18 and over, and Overanxious Disorder for those under 18.

ANXIETY DISORDERS (or Anxiety and Phobic Neuroses)

The Anxiety Disorders, which are not specifically related to children, include the Phobic Disorders. The subtypes applicable to the childhood and adolescent years are listed in Table 32. For a comprehensive review of diagnostic and treatment issues for anxiety disorders in children and adolescents, see Leonard & Rapoport (in press).

Panic Disorder with Agoraphobia or Agoraphobia Without a History of Panic Attacks is presumed to be linked with childhood Separation

TABLE 32
Anxiety Disorders: DSM-III-R Axis I Codes

300.23	Social Phobia
	Specify if generalized
300.29	Simple Phobia
300.01	Panic Disorder, Without Agoraphobia
300.30	Obsessive Compulsive Disorder
309.89	Post-traumatic Stress Disorder
	Specify if delayed onset
300.02	Generalized Anxiety Disorder
300.00	Anxiety Disorder NOS

Anxiety Disorder, although onset is usually not until late adolescence or early adulthood. The following discussion highlights important features of these anxiety disorders as applied to the pediatric population.

Phobic Disorders

These subtypes involved a specific stimulus which, when encountered, initiates the anxiety response. Symptoms also include the avoidance of the stimulus situations, objects, or activities that set off the anxiety response. Even though the subject may recognize the disproportionate emotion associated with the stimulus, continued and irrational avoidance of the anxiety source interferes with social and occupational functioning. When more than one type is present, multiple diagnoses are given.

Social Phobia. The common element of this phobia is a desire to protect oneself from situations in which others have the opportunity to observe and includes most social situations. Such exposure to the view of others creates a continual fear of and wish to avoid such occasions because of possible humiliation and embarrassment. In DSM-III-R the definition is expanded and clarified such that significant interference with functioning and/or distress must occur. The individual usually fears only one type of situation and recognizes the irrationality of the fear and consequent reaction. Anticipatory anxiety only strengthens phobic avoidance. In most instances the course is chronic, but rarely incapacitating. The disorder is not associated with Major Depression, nor is it diagnosed in cases of Schizophrenia, Obsessive Compulsive Disorder, Simple Phobia, or Paranoid Personality Disorder. For children and adolescents, Avoidant Disorder of Childhood or Adolescence preempts this diagnosis. However, an associated diagnosis of Avoidant Personality Disorder can be made at any age.

Simple Phobia. The phobic reaction in this disorder is not attributable to potentially embarrassing or humiliating social situations, as in Social Phobia, or a fear of being alone or away from home, as in Panic Disorder with Agoraphobia. The most common phobic stimuli encountered in individuals with this disorder are animals and heights or closed spaces. In all instances the disturbance is recognized as unreasonable distress and is not attributable to any other mental disorder. The diagnosis would not be used in cases of Schizophrenia. The differential diagnosis from Obsessive Compulsive Disorder may be difficult, but the content of obsessive anxiety, which usually focuses on dirt, illness, or other danger, usually permits differentiation.

Panic Disorder Without Agoraphobia. The diagnosis requires at least four unpredictable recurring attacks of extreme anxiety within a four-week period, or one or more attacks followed by at least a month of fear of having another attack. Although certain situations may be associated with the attack, the episode is not viewed as a response to a recognizable stimulus. Onset is characterized by intense feelings of terror, apprehension, and impending doom. Anxiety symptoms experienced during the panic attack are outlined in DSM-III-R; four of them must be apparent for the diagnosis. The attack usually lasts several minutes, more rarely a couple of hours, but nervousness and apprehension, accompanied by physiological symptoms, may persist following the attack. The course is variable, in both length and severity. Sudden object loss is thought to be a predisposing factor, and a history of Separation Anxiety Disorder may indicate susceptibility.

Panic Disorder can occur in early adolescence but is quite rare. Differential considerations include the context of the complaint, as similar symptoms may arise after extreme physical exertion or a life-threatening event, in which case a diagnosis is not designated. Some physical disorders (e.g., hyperthyroidism), as well as withdrawal or intoxication from certain substances, may also simulate symptoms. The diagnosis is also not given when panic attacks occur in conjunction with major mental disorders (e.g., Schizophrenia, Major Depression, or Somatization Disorder). Generalized Anxiety Disorder is dismissed if there is evidence of panic attacks by history, although there may be some similarity initially because of the pervasive anxious quality that is evident in the interlude between episodes. In Panic Disorder, the anxiety attack may be provoked without encountering a known stimulus, and it is this quality which distinguishes it from Panic Attack With Agoraphobia, and Simple or Social Phobia.

Obsessive Compulsive Disorder. Diagnosis of this disorder specifies the persistence of either *obsessions* or *compulsions*, although the two frequently occur simultaneously. Obsessions are ego-dystonic thoughts that are recurrent and persistent even when attempts are made to ignore them. Compulsions are comprised of intentional, repetitive activities or behaviors engaged in so that some effect is obtained or consequence is prevented, although no realistic causal relationship exists between the behavior and the construed event. Resistance to the compulsion results in increased tension, which dissipates after engaging in the compulsion. Obsessions and compulsions are sufficiently severe and time consuming to interfere with social, academic, and/or occupational functioning and cause the individual marked distress by interfering with normal routines, job or academic performance, and interpersonal relationships. The condition is not attributable to another existing mental disorder such as Tourette's Disorder, Schizophrenia, Major Depression, or an Organic Mental Disorder. It is distinguished from Disorders of Impulse Control Not Elsewhere Classified in that in the latter conditions, the nature of the activity itself provides some degree of pleasure or release.

Onset is in adolescence or early adulthood in the majority of cases, and it occurs more frequently in childhood than had been thought, possibly in excess of 1% occurrence in an adolescent epidemiological study (Flament et al., 1988). Childhood cases closely resemble the adult clinical picture. Recovery rate may be only 50%, however, for adolescents as well as adults (Rapoport, 1989), a fact that merits increased efforts on the part of clinicians to make early identification and initiate interventive treatment in understanding this chronic and incapacitating illness. The disorder is often only elicited by direct questions about rituals or obsessive thoughts. Depressive symptoms are common, but in childhood and adolescence, the onset of depression usually occurs after onset of obsessive compulsive symptoms. Both diagnoses should be used if diagnostic criteria are met. Substance abuse is an additional complication often associated with the disorder.

Post-traumatic Stress Disorder. This category warrants a brief comment if only to stress the importance of differential diagnosis. This subtype is provided for reactions to situations of extreme stress and psychological trauma that are beyond the range of normal human experience. The DSM-III-R criteria have been made more age-appropriate, allowing, for example, for repetitive play in young children in which themes or aspects of the trauma are considered in experiencing the traumatic event. In young children, loss of recently acquired developmental skills, for example, toilet training, may be considered equivalent to the adult symptom of numbing of general responsiveness. Post-traumatic Stress Disorder may prove to be an important research area for child psychiatry; one study of Vietnam veterans has suggested, for example, that persons in late adolescence in comparison with young adulthood may be relatively prone to Post-traumatic Stress Disorder (van der Kolk, 1985). Adjustment Disorder rarely involves a stressor of equal magnitude and the quality of reliving the trauma is absent. Similarly, problems that might be coded under V Codes (e.g., Uncomplicated Bereavement, Phase of Life Problem) may be described as traumatic stress but are within the range of everyday human experience. Duration must be for at least one month. Specify delayed onset, if symptoms did not occur until at least six months after the trauma.

Anxiety Disorder NOS. This subtype is used for those instances of Anxiety Disorder or phobic avoidance that do not meet criteria for the other specified illnesses. Careful documentation and comparison with the other categories are the only way such a category will be helpful to future study of these disorders.

Comment on Anxiety Disorders:
Their Diagnosis in Children and Adolescents
Anxiety Disorders are more prevalent in childhood than had been thought previously (Flament et al., 1988; Gittelman, 1986). DSM-III-R has "tightened up" some of the diagnoses, but how Generalized Anxiety Disorder and Social Phobia are to be specifically distinguished in childhood remains unclear. In addition, the equivalence of childhood and adult Anxiety Disorders is unclear, as long-term prospective studies of these childhood disorders are lacking. Finally, pilot data suggest that too many pediatric cases under clinical treatment for "anxiety" may not meet criteria for any one of the disorders, having only one or more symptoms of several different disorders (R. Gittelman, personal communication). Such an undifferentiated group will need more careful study.

The DSM-III-R refinement of the category of Anxiety Disorders of Childhood or Adolescence is a useful step, furthering research on fundamental questions of equivalence between childhood and adult disorders, e.g., Separation Anxiety Disorder and Agoraphobia, Overanxious Disorder and Generalized Anxiety Disorder, and so forth. Major problems remain, however. The Anxiety Disorders have proven to be the most difficult group to diagnose reliably both in DSM-III field trials and in later more focused research (Prendergast et al., 1988; Gittelman, 1986). While DSM-III-R more clearly specifies particular symptoms than any system to date, it is probable that structured interviews will still be particularly important for achieving reliability. Except for severe cases, this is the most problematic patient group diagnostically.

CASE HISTORIES

Alex
Alex is a 13-year-old boy referred by his psychiatrist for "compulsions." About six months ago, he began laying out his clothes and smoothing

them for several minutes before putting them on; then he would open and close the dresser drawers. Three months later he began putting on and taking off his pants several times. A month ago he had to say where he was going eight times, after which his mother had to say "OK"; otherwise he would feel frustrated and repeat himself again. At school he opened and closed his locker door repeatedly. On arriving home, he had to enter and exit the house three or four times to touch his bicycle left outside. For the past five months, he has avoided stepping on sidewalk cracks. He has always been shy, but three or four months ago he stopped seeing his few friends.

Compulsion did not appear until this year. At age three, however, his parents had to say "Goodnight" 10 or 12 times before he could sleep. This need lasted only a few months. At age eight he told his mother he had a "radio" in his head. The radio spoke in complete sentences, telling him to do good things. He enjoyed listening to it. It lasted for a year and he wishes it "would come back."

About the same time his rituals started this year, his speech became quieter and murmuring. Three months ago he began to stop in midsentence, leaving out pronouns and prepositions. According to his mother, he can still speak in complete sentences when relaxed. He also blurts out irrelevant statements in class, although they may have been relevant to previously addressed subjects, and has episodes of unprovoked silly laughter or tearfulness, which he can't stop.

Medical examination revealed a mild-standing head tumor and some fidgetiness. The patient had been off thioridazine for a month. An EEG is described as abnormal with paroxysmal bursts of activity.

During the psychiatric interview the patient was cooperative; however, he repeatedly pulled on his upper lip and seemed to fidget. Affect was shallow, narrow, stable, and occasionally inappropriate. Mood was mostly apathetic. He occasionally smiled or giggled for no reason, but denied perceptual disturbances or delusions. He was fully oriented. Concentration and intermediate memory were good. Speech was asyndetic and contained instances of blocking, derailment, and telegraphic speech perseveration, as well as delayed and immediate echolalia.

Diagnosis

Axis I:	298.90 Psychotic Disorder NOS (Atypical Psychosis)
Axis II:	None
Axis III:	Possible Seizure Disorder
	Possible Tardive Dyskinesia

Axis IV: Severity: 1—None
          Stressor(s): N/A
Axis V: Current GAF: 75
          Highest GAF past year: 80

Discussion

Alex initially presented in a manner resembling Obsessive Compulsive Disorder. However, the bizarre behavior and increasingly obvious thought disorder make the diagnosis of Atypical Psychosis most apparent. It may be argued that Alex's condition is progressively advancing toward Schizophrenia, Disorganized Type (295.1x), but to the child psychiatrists seeing the patient early in the disorder, this is less apparent. The blocking and difficulty speaking suggest absence seizures to the neurologist, and a trial of antiepileptic medication is being undertaken.

Laura

Laura, aged nine, was brought to the clinic for excessive shyness, difficulty going to sleep, and inability to be alone in the house. In addition, she had begun to brood that the family dog would get sick and die. Her mother had just returned home following three months of psychiatric hospitalization for severe Depression. The mother's illness had followed her husband's (Laura's father's) separation from the family in order to live with another woman whom he intended to marry.

Laura had been reluctant to attend school when in kindergarten and first grade, but this had been handled by the school by just setting limits about school attendance. At home, she often slept in her parents' bed.

In the past two years, the problems had worsened considerably. Frequently, Laura would fake illness on school days, and she had begun to do poorly academically. Recent testing had revealed reading difficulties that were thought to be long standing, and tutoring had been instated. This academic year she was repeating third grade. Laura had taken this poorly and had no friends.

During the psychiatric interview, Laura spoke with reluctance and appeared sad. She seemed preoccupied with her dog Mandy and feared that the dog might fall ill. When asked directly, she said she did not sleep well unless she was in the same bed as her mother. Although she admitted she could not stay in the house alone even for 10 minutes, she claimed this was almost never a problem as long as her older sister, a neighbor, or a housekeeper was with her—which was almost all the time. She admitted she wanted to have more friends but was reluctant to spend much time at their houses except for a girl who lived next door from whose house she could see her own.

Diagnosis

Axis I:	309.21 Separation Anxiety Disorder
Axis II:	315.00 Developmental Reading Disorder
Axis III:	None
Axis IV:	Severity: 4—Moderate (Predominantly enduring circumstances)
	Stressor(s): Parental separation, mother's depression and hospitalization
Axis V:	Current GAF: 60
	Highest GAF past year: 60

Discussion

Laura, like many children with Anxiety Disorders, has elements that resemble a Mood Disorder (insomnia, sadness, isolation). Her preoccupation with her dog's possible illness had suggested the possibility of Obsessive Compulsive Disorder. At times the intensity of her concern about her dog's illness raised the possibility of a thought disorder, but Laura's otherwise sensible behavior and good interpersonal skills on interview argued against this. The chronicity of her symptoms had made the diagnosis of Adjustment Reaction untenable.

Chapter 14

Disorders Manifesting
a Physical Nature

These disorders—Eating Disorders, Tic Disorders, Stereotypy/Habit Disorder, Speech Disorders Not Elsewhere Classified, Elimination Disorders, and Sleep Disorders—demonstrate fairly straightforward symptom patterns characterized by specific physical impairment.

DSM-III-R has somewhat rearranged disorders that we have kept together in this chapter. Stereotypy/Habit Disorder has been separated from the Tic Disorders in the appropriate recognition that such disparate behaviors as self-mutilation, head banging, and nail biting have quite different significance and patterns of association from those of Tic Disorders. Unfortunately, Sleepwalking and Sleep Terror Disorder have been moved to a separate Sleep Disorders section in spite of their predominant occurrence in childhood. Equally confusing is the fact that the Speech Disorders, Stuttering and Cluttering, are coded on Axis I whereas other Speech Disorders are coded on Axis II under the Specific Developmental Disorders.

EATING DISORDERS
Each of the five subtypes of Eating Disorders is characterized by gross alterations in eating behavior. Of the five, Pica and Rumination usually occur during infancy and early childhood, and the others are typically adolescent phenomena. Rumination and Anorexia Nervosa may progress to death.

TABLE 33
Eating Disorders: DSM-III-R Axis I Codes

307.10   Anorexia Nervosa
307.51   Bulimia Nervosa
307.52   Pica
307.53   Rumination Disorder of Infancy
307.50   Eating Disorder NOS

Anorexia Nervosa

The essential feature of Anorexia Nervosa is an intense fear of becoming obese, accompanied by significant and excessive weight loss, which is not associated with any physical disorder. It most frequently occurs in females between the ages of 12 and 18 and is a relatively common diagnosis. Accompanying symptoms include disturbed body image, refusal to gain weight, and amenorrhea in females. The DSM-III-R criteria specify a weight loss of at least 15% of original body weight or, if under age 18, 15% under expected weight as determined by growth charts, and absence of at least three menstrual cycles.

The diagnosis is unlikely to present a problem, as weight loss in Major Depression or Obsessive Compulsive Disorder is seldom as profound and is not associated with a fear of becoming fat. In Schizophrenia, atypical eating patterns may be evident, but other psychotic symptoms are seldom associated with Anorexia Nervosa. It is possible, however, for this condition to be diagnosed in addition to Schizophrenia or Major Depression.

Bulimia Nervosa

Bulimia Nervosa is being recognized with increasing frequency. It is identified by episodic binge eating and preoccupation with this abnormal eating pattern. The individual may experience alternate periods of rabid craving and great concern over inability to stop overeating. There may be vomiting between episodes or laxative abuse. Depression and self-critical thoughts usually follow the binges. There is no evidence of a physical cause for the disorder. It should be differentiated from Anorexia Nervosa, as some anorexics also have bulimic episodes. In Bulimia Nervosa, there may be weight fluctuation and overemphasis on eating, but weight loss is never as severe as in Anorexia Nervosa.

Pica

Persistent consumption of nonnutritive substances such as dirt, plaster, hair, bugs, and/or pebbles characterizes this disorder. There is no aversion to food. Onset is usually between 12 and 24 months of age, with remission in childhood. Pica rarely persists into adolescence or adulthood. The problem is more common in children who are poorly supervised or retarded. The DSM-III-R criteria specify that it is not due to another mental disorder, such as Autistic Disorder or Schizophrenia, or to a physical disorder (e.g., Kleine-Levin syndrome).

Rumination Disorder of Infancy

Rumination is a well-defined syndrome. Although it was first described in adult patients, it is much more common in children. The essential feature is repeated regurgitation of partially digested food, which is then chewed, spit out, or swallowed without nausea, retching, or other signs of gastro-intestinal distress. The condition is potentially fatal because of weight loss or no weight gain and subsequent malnutrition. The infant may find that the process of bringing the food into the mouth is pleasurable. The disorder may begin at three to 12 months of age, though onset is later in retarded infants. Physical examination rules out possible physiological factors that may contribute to the symptoms. "Psychogenic" and "Self-stimulating" subtypes have been proposed for normal and retarded patients, respectively, but such a distinction has yet to be replicated (Dickerson et al., 1988).

CASE HISTORIES

Robert

Robert was admitted to the pediatric ward at eight months of age with principal complaint of failure to gain weight. His mother was also concerned about his persistent odor. Development had been normal up to the age of six months. During the subsequent months he had begun to display a peculiar behavior after each feeding. He would sit up, his head high and neck arched back, open his mouth until milk appeared, then either reswallow it or let it dribble down his chin. The milk seemed to be the source of Robert's very sour smell. The mother was unmarried, living with different relatives for periods at a time, which meant that Robert had been handed around to several different caretakers. Baby Robert, however, appeared content, smiled readily, and was reportedly easy to care for.

Diagnosis

Axis I:	307.53 Rumination Disorder of Infancy
Axis II:	V71.09 No diagnosis on Axis II
Axis III:	None
Axis IV:	Severity: 4 — Moderate (Predominantly enduring circumstances)
	Stressor(s): Inconsistent care
Axis V:	Current GAF: 60
	Highest GAF past year: Not applicable

Discussion

Robert manifests all of the features of Rumination Disorder of Infancy. He proved unusually difficult to feed, however, as special caretaking, increased attention, and feeding with very thick cereal were not successful. He finally responded to adverse conditioning. Mild electric shocks were applied to his leg when he displayed ruminating behaviors. With one week of this treatment he stopped ruminating and was still well at one-year follow-up. Here, an Axis IV that named psychosocial stressors would be more informative.

Deborah

Deborah, a 15-year-old girl who lives with her parents, asked to be seen because of binge eating and vomiting. Her weight ranged from 160 pounds when she was 14 to a low of 125. She has a tendency to be slightly chubby; she is only 5'2". At age 12 she started bingeing and vomiting. She is an excellent athlete, jogs six to eight miles a day, and plays competitive basketball at her high school.

There are periods when she feels depressed, mainly because of friction at home between her parents. She is more likely to binge during these times, eating in secret, usually junk food, but it can be anything available, including an entire roast chicken or several sandwiches. At other times, however, the bingeing will start when things are relatively calm. She then becomes depressed about how fat she looks and refuses dates because of her embarrassment. She may binge several times a week for months and then resume periods of normal eating.

She is a good student and is curious about the psychological basis for her bingeing. She says she now understands how an alcoholic must feel (she has no interest in alcohol), because she knows the eating is bad for her but she simply can't stop when she starts bingeing.

Diagnosis
Axis I:	307.51 Bulimia Nervosa
Axis II:	V71.09 No diagnosis on Axis II
Axis III:	None
Axis IV:	Severity: 4—Moderate (Predominantly enduring circumstances)
	Stressor(s): Hostile relationship between parents
Axis V:	Current GAF: 65
	Highest GAF past year: 70

Discussion
Deborah is typical of many bulimics with onset in adolescence, sometimes but not invariably associated with depressed mood. Enormous quantities of food are consumed, often secretly, with large fluctuation in body weight. Although Bulimia Nervosa can be associated with Anorexia Nervosa, there is no evidence of this here, as Deborah has never been thin. It might be reasonable to add the diagnosis of Adjustment Disorder with Depressed Mood if the nature of the stressor was more extreme, but it would not add substantially since depression, at least mild depression, is usually associated with Bulimia Nervosa. A diagnosis of Major Depression is not made in this case because depressive symptoms are not severe enough to interfere with overall functioning. Because Bulimia Nervosa may be episodic, patients may be seen during periods where they do not technically meet the minimum criteria (twice weekly) for diagnosis. In the (many) cases where this is true, a diagnosis of Eating Disorder Not Otherwise Specified will be used.

Roger
Roger, a two-year-old black boy, was brought to the clinic by his mother because of stomach pains. He has been slow to develop, sitting at one year of age and walking at 20 months. In addition, he is somewhat small for his age. During the many hours that Roger is left unattended in the family yard, he has been seen to pick up and eat dirt, sand, bugs, and leaves. He often vomits these substances, but then resumes eating. He has had constipation and pain before.

During hospital admission, he received a lot of attention from the ward nurses because he was "cute and friendly." While in the hospital, he showed no tendency to eat nonnutritive substances. There was apprehension about returning him home, however, where the supervision was poor (by a mentally retarded grandmother who herself is said to eat plaster).

Diagnosis

Axis I:	307.52 Pica
Axis II:	319.00 Unspecified Mental Retardation
Axis III:	None
Axis IV:	Severity: 4 — Moderate (Predominantly enduring circumstances)
	Stressor(s): Insufficient parental care
Axis V:	Current: 45
	Past year: 45

Discussion

Bizarre eating patterns can occur with psychosis but Roger displays no evidence of this, nor does he fit the description of Autistic Disorder (friendly, language not specifically delayed). Pica is frequently associated with Mental Retardation, which is suspected because of the slow development. The lack of supervision and even the familial pattern are considered typical.

Kathy

Kathy, a 15-year-old girl, was referred for an initial evaluation to an outpatient therapist because of preoccupation with exercise and weight loss. During the following six months, she went from her usual weight of 125 pounds to 90 pounds, at which point she was hospitalized. During hospitalization, she was irritable, denied having a problem, and volunteered for patient activities involving food, that is, cooking for ward parties, and so on. She was polite and superficially cooperative on the ward, although food intake had to be monitored carefully because of her ingenious ways of disposing of food. She was amenorrheic. During hospitalization, she was noted to have many obsessive ideas, such as feeling she must walk in a certain rhythm, and she felt compelled to follow routines. These interfered slightly with her recreational activities.

Her parents reported that she was even-tempered, well behaved, and almost "too good" as a child. Before becoming ill, she had been a good student and had had a few close friends.

She was discharged at a weight of 100 pounds and has been stable at about 105 pounds in outpatient therapy.

Diagnosis

Axis I:	307.10 Anorexia Nervosa
Axis II:	V71.09 No diagnosis on Axis II
Axis III:	None
Axis IV:	Severity: 1—None
	Stressor(s): N/A
Axis V:	Current GAF: 80
	Highest GAF past year: 80

Discussion

Kathy presents a typical picture of Anorexia Nervosa. There is seldom difficulty with this diagnosis because of the preoccupation with weight and profound weight loss in the absence of physical illness. The excessive exercise, interest in food, and compulsive traits are also commonly associated. The case is slightly unusual in the relative absence of associated depression, although she was irritable on the ward.

TIC DISORDERS

The presenting feature of all Tic Disorders is an abnormality of gross motor movement. These disorders include Transient Tics, Chronic Motor or Vocal Tics, and Tourette's Syndrome. Any association between the disorders is, as yet, unknown, but they may all be variations of one disorder.

Tics account for only approximately 5% of cases referred to child guidance clinics, but they have received considerable interest of late in terms of the amount of distress caused the child and the efficacy of drug treatment for Tourette's Disorder. Appearing primarily in the upper portion of the face, tics resemble patterns of startle response. They are defined as involuntary and rapid movement of a group of functionally related

TABLE 34
Tic Disorders: DSM-III-R Axis I Codes

307.21	Transient Tic Disorder
307.22	Chronic Motor or Vocal Tic Disorder
307.23	Tourette's Disorder
307.20	Tic Disorder NOS

Under Other Disorders of Infancy, Childhood, or Adolescence
307.30   Stereotypy/Habit Disorder

skeletal muscles or involuntary production of sounds or words. These characteristics distinguish tics from other involuntary movement disorders: choreiform, dystonic, athetoid, and myoclonic movements, as well as other, more rare neurological conditions such as hemiballismus. Spasms are differentiated by slower, more prolonged disturbance involving groups of muscles. Tics must also be distinguished from dyskinesias, which are silent oral-buccal-lingual movements and limb movements.

Tic Disorders arise most commonly in early childhood, with average age of onset at seven years, and only rarely in adolescence. They are more common in males of average or above average intelligence, a factor contributing to diagnostic distinction from stereotypies of the mentally retarded. Both emotional and hysterical qualities have been cited as possible precipitating factors; however, few emotional causes have been linked to these disorders. Although stress may exacerbate tics, occurrence during tranquil periods of life is just as typical of the symptom course. A minority of cases support association with symptoms of emotional disturbance, for example, anxiety; there are, however, few instances of association with behavior disorders. Attention-Deficit Hyperactivity Disorder, on the other hand, is a frequent presenting problem or associated condition with Tourette's Disorder. Familial patterns have also been reported for all forms of Tic Disorders, although nonfamilial cases are most commonly encountered. Evidence of nervous system "immaturity" or early pre- and perinatal insult has been documented, but the association is not striking.

Accompanying features often include considerable self-consciousness and secondary symptoms of depression. Both social and academic functioning may suffer as a result of the severity of the tic in combination with self-consciousness on the part of the patient and those interacting with him or her.

Transient Tic Disorder
Transient Tic Disorder must have its onset during early childhood or adolescence; cases have been reported as early as two years of age. The recurrence of the involuntary motor or vocal tics can be voluntarily suppressed for a period of time up to several hours. The intensity of the symptoms can vary over a period of weeks or months, but the criteria for the Transient Tic Disorder require duration for at least two weeks but not more than one year. Eye blinks or other facial tics are most common, but limbs or torso may also be involved and in rare cases vocal tics may also occur. The tics may disappear but typically recur and worsen during periods of stress. Transient tics are common and may occur in 10% to 20%

of school-aged children. Differential diagnosis is evaluated in terms of chronicity or development of Tourette's Disorder.

Chronic Motor or Vocal Tic Disorder

Chronic Motor or Vocal Tic Disorder is very similar to Transient Tic Disorder, with the exception that the intensity of symptoms is constant over weeks or months and duration exceeds one year. Vocal tics are unusual and, if persistent, indicate Tourette's Disorder.

Chronic tics usually begin in childhood, have a chronic course, and tend to be limited to no more than three particular muscle groups. They are also thought to be more common in males.

Transient Tic Disorder differs from Chronic Motor Tic Disorder in intensity and duration of the disturbance, while in Tourette's Disorder intensity may vary over time, vocal tics are much more prominent, and motor movements tend to be brief and weak compared to those in Chronic Motor Tic Disorder.

Tourette's Disorder

The essential features once again involve involuntary repetitive motor movements, but these must be accompanied by vocal tics. Motor tics involve the head and may include other parts of the body as well, particularly the torso and upper limbs. Vocal tics include various sounds, such as grunts, yelps, sniffs, coughs, or words. Coprolalia, the involuntary uttering of obscenities, is present in 60% of the cases. Tics may be voluntarily suppressed for minutes or hours and vary in intensity. Duration of more than one year is required for diagnosis.

Associated features include imitation of observed motions (echokinesis), repeating what one has just said (palilalia), mental corprolalia, obsessive thoughts, compulsions to touch things, or impulsive performance of complicated movements. The disorder may appear by age two and is almost always present by age 13; diagnostic criteria indicate a cutoff age of 21 years. It is three times more common in boys than in girls and occurrence among family members is more frequent than in the general population.

Tic Disorder NOS

This category is for tics that do not meet the criteria for classification in the previous categories.

Stereotypy/Habit Disorder

Although not classified as a Tic Disorder, this category is indicated for conditions involving voluntary and nonspasmodic movement which may or may not have associated distress accompanying the symptoms. Such conditions are found almost exclusively in children and may include head banging, repetitive hand movement, or rocking. DSM-III-R also includes very excessive nail biting and skin picking. Incidence is especially prevalent in children with Mental Retardation and Pervasive Developmental Disorder, is common in those lacking adequate social stimulation, and may also occur in absence of mental disorder.

CASE HISTORY

David
Nine-year-old David had been receiving outpatient treatment at a child guidance clinic for two years because of hyperactive, inattentive, and immature behavior. For about a year he had been tried on stimulant medication, which was helpful in controlling his behavior. However, while on stimulants he began to develop facial tics and had throat clearing. The tics continued even when stimulants were discontinued. The throat clearing had originally been ascribed to allergy; however, it progressed over the following year to grunts, and the facial tics were eventually accompanied by jerks of the shoulder.

Diagnosis
Axis I:	307.23 Tourette's Disorder
Axis II:	V71.09 No diagnosis on Axis II
Axis III:	None
Axis IV:	0 — Inadequate information
	Stressor(s): N/A
Axis V:	Current GAF: 60
	Highest GAF past year: 60

Discussion
This patient's history is typical of that of about 50% of males with Tourette's Disorder, including a prior diagnosis or symptom pattern of Attention-Deficit Hyperactivity Disorder. The role of stimulants in the onset of this disorder is not clear; however, for at least some patients this type of medication seems to aggravate the syndrome. An additional diagnosis of Attention-Deficit Hyperactivity Disorder was not made in this case, although for many patients with Tourette's, the restless and inattentive behavior of Attention-Deficit Hyperactivity Disorder may be

the most difficult aspect of the patient's condition. The degree of association between cases referred for treatment of Attention-Deficit Hyperactivity Disorder and the subsequent diagnosis of Tourette's Disorder remains controversial, but some association is generally assumed and is striking in clinical populations.

OTHER DISORDERS WITH PHYSICAL MANIFESTATIONS

These disorders affect physical functioning in the areas of excretion, speech, and sleep. Psychological conflict was formerly thought to be the cause of these conditions; however, few children with these specific disorders have associated mental disturbance.

Functional Enuresis

Diagnostic indications are a continued pattern of involuntary or intentional voiding of urine not accounted for by physical disorder and occurring after the age at which continence is expected. If bladder control has not been established prior to onset, the disorder is called *primary;* otherwise, onset after a one-year period of continence is referred to as *secondary.* No means for coding this distinction has been provided. An age criterion specifies that in five- and six-year-olds occurrence is two times per month and in older children it is once a month. Functional Encopresis, Sleepwalking Disorder, and Sleep Terror Disorder are also reported as accompanying complaints.

TABLE 35
Other Disorders with Physical Manifestations: DSM-III-R Axis I Codes

Elimination Disorders
307.60   Functional Enuresis
307.70   Functional Encopresis
         Specify nocturnal only, diurnal only, or nocturnal and diurnal

Speech Disorders Not Elsewhere Classified
307.00   Stuttering
307.00   Cluttering

Sleep Disorders (Parsomnias)
307.46   Sleepwalking Disorder
307.46   Sleep Terror Disorder

Functional Encopresis

In this disorder the distinction between *primary* and *secondary* occurrence is also made, but no code is specified. Its prominent characteristic is the voluntary or involuntary passage of feces in places that are inappropriate for the social and cultural background of the child, which occurs at least once a month for a minimal period of six months. The involuntary/voluntary distinction is associated with contributing factors, such as constipation or retention in the case of involuntary passage of feces. Antisocial or psychopathological processes may be behind deliberate incontinence. Physical disorder or severe Mental Retardation must be ruled out for the diagnosis. The diagnosis would not be made in children under four years of age.

Stuttering

Stuttering or stammering is characterized by prolonged repetition of sounds and syllables, abnormal hesitations and pauses, all of which disrupt normal speech rhythms. There may be accompanying jerks, blinks, and tremors; extent of the disturbance typically varies by situation. Onset is usually before age 12 and course is often chronic with periods of remission. In mild cases, over 50% recovery is reported.

Cluttering

This category, new to DSM-III-R, indicates a disorder of speech rate and rhythm that impairs intelligibility. Speech is erratic and jerky, with bursts of speech unrelated to grammatical structure of the sentence. This has the same code as Stuttering.

Sleepwalking Disorder and Sleep Terror Disorder

Sleepwalking and Sleep Terror Disorders (both coded as 307.46) are part of a new Sleep Disorders section of DSM-III-R. They are presented here, however, because of the large number of pediatric patients with these disorders.

Sleepwalking Disorder is diagnosed on report of repeated episodes when the individual rises from bed and walks about. He/she is nonresponsive to others during this time and later has no recollection of the event. At the time of occurrence, it is nearly impossible to rouse the individual. After awakening, there is no evidence of impaired mental activity or of behavior, though a brief period of confusion or disorientation may initially ensue. There is no evidence of abnormal brain activity during sleep or that the episode occurs specifically during REM sleep.

Sleep Terror Disorder is described as a pattern of incidents typified by abrupt awakening, usually preceded by a panicky scream, with evidence of intense anxiety apparent throughout the episode. There is relative unresponsiveness to others during the occurrence, at which time the person appears confused and disoriented and exhibits, at times, perseverative motions. No evidence of abnormal brain activity or REM sleep is linked to the episode.

There is no association between these disturbances and any other mental disorder. Epileptic seizure activity would rule out these diagnoses. Sleep Terror Disorder has a different quality than nightmares, in which the anxiety experience is mild and the person is able to recall most or all portions of the dream sequence.

Chapter 15

Other Disorders of Infancy, Childhood, or Adolescence

This section reviews DSM-III-R disorders that include a group of newer disorders for which there was no counterpart in DSM-II and which are still evolving. Some of these disorders were suited for placement within other major categories for convenience of discussion or to point out diagnostic differences. Reactive Attachment Disorder of Infancy or Childhood found a place in Chapter 9 (Developmental Abnormalities in the First Years of Life), Stereotypy/Habit Disorder has been discussed in Chapter 14 (Disorders Manifesting a Physical Nature), and Undifferentiated Attention-Deficit Disorder was listed with the Disruptive Behavior Disorders (Chapter 12). A brief discussion of Adjustment Disorders is added in this chapter, since this category deserves comment for use with children and adolescents. In addition, Gender Identity Disorders are discussed here. This new category in the DSM-III-R reorganization was placed under the childhood disorders section in recognition that the onset of these disorders occurs primarily in childhood or adolescence.

OTHER DISORDERS OF INFANCY, CHILDHOOD, OR ADOLESCENCE

Elective Mutism
The essential aspect in Elective Mutism is the refusal to speak in almost all situations, despite adequate speech and language development and com-

prehension. A child with this disorder may at times communicate through gestures and other nonverbal communication. The refusal to speak is not due to another mental disorder or to any developmental disability, even though there is reported incidence of delayed language development or articulation difficulties.

Associated behavioral disturbance is often observed, particularly negativism and oppositional behavior. The disorder usually comes to the attention of school personnel initially, due to academic underachievement or failure and social ostracism. What little research there is points to continued behavioral difficulties, even when speech is resumed.

Differential diagnoses are Severe or Profound Mental Retardation, Pervasive Developmental Disorders, or Developmental Language Disorder. A general refusal to speak may also be apparent in cases of Major Depression, Avoidant Disorder of Childhood or Adolescence, Overanxious Disorder, Oppositional Defiant Disorder, and Social Phobia. None of these disorders manifests a prominent lack of speech, however, and intellectual testing and general psychiatric evaluation will quickly point out these distinctions. Excessively shy children or children from families who speak a different language from that of the dominant culture may also present with speech refusal.

Identity Disorder

The debilitating feature of this disorder is succinctly summarized by the question "Who am I?" Identity Disorder originates in the subject's inability to reconcile a variety of issues and integrate a coherent and acceptable sense of self. As a result, academic, social, and occupational functioning are impaired, with varying degree of severity, for a period of more than three months. Onset typically occurs in late adolescence.

TABLE 36
Other Disorders of Infancy, Childhood, or Adolescence: DSM-III-R Axis I Codes

313.23	Elective Mutism
313.82	Identity Disorder
313.89*	Reactive Attachment Disorder of Infancy or Early Childhood
307.30*	Stereotypy/Habit Disorder
314.00*	Undifferentiated Attention-Deficit Disorder

*Codes included in the DSM-III-R section but discussed elsewhere.

Differential consideration evaluates the degree to which the conflict deviates from the normal process of maturing and separation from the family constellation. Severity of the distress and ensuing impairment offer guidelines for determining this deviation. Diagnosis of Schizophrenia, Schizophreniform Disorder, or Mood Disorder preempts consideration of Identity Disorder as a diagnosis.

Borderline Personality Disorder is considered if the patient is over age 18; however, its particular characteristics involve several areas of impairment, and disturbance of mood is prominent. In such cases, when the latter criteria are met, this diagnosis would be used in place of Identity Disorder.

There is an uncertain relationship between incidence of Identity Disorder in adolescence and appearance of more severe forms of mental disorder later in life. Identity Disorder remains a controversial category.

ADJUSTMENT DISORDERS

Adjustment Disorders are not placed under the Childhood Disorders section of DSM-III-R; however, because this diagnosis is used to a considerable extent by child psychiatrists, it is discussed here.

The essential feature of an Adjustment Disorder is that there is a maladaptive reaction that occurs *within three months* of the onset of a stressor. Such stressors may include changing schools, parental separation, or illness in the family. In terms of severity, Adjustment Disorders fall in between V Code conditions, where there is no maladaptive behavior, and the more severe disorders. For example, if criteria for Major Depression or

TABLE 37
Adjustment Disorders: DSM-III-R Axis I Codes

309.24	with Anxious Mood
309.00	with Depressed Mood
309.30	with Disturbance of Conduct
309.40	with Mixed Disturbance of Emotions and Conduct
309.28	with Mixed Emotional Features
309.82	with Physical Complaints
309.83	with Withdrawal
309.23	with Work (or Academic) Inhibition
309.90	Adjustment Disorder Not Otherwise Specified

Conduct Disorder are fulfilled, then Adjustment Disorder should not be used. DSM-III-R specifies that duration longer than six months precludes this diagnosis. One of the advantages of a multiaxial scheme is that Axis I is for description alone, and Axis IV can be used to record psychosocial stressors. Therefore, even if the criteria for a major disorder are met, there are still ways of recording the pertinent stressor. Since both the pattern of maladaptive behavior and the stressor have been recorded, different patterns of behavioral reaction can be compared on follow-up.

GENDER IDENTITY DISORDERS
The grouping of Gender Identity Disorders within the childhood disorder section acknowledges the almost universal onset of these disorders in childhood or adolescence; these issues rarely develop for the first time in adult life.

Gender Identity Disorder of Childhood
This disorder is typified by incongruence between gender identity and anatomical sex. Definition of gender identity is related to public expression of gender role, which in turn is influenced by individual perception of gender.

In Gender Identity Disorder of Childhood, symptoms are characterized by a persistent discomfort with anatomical sex and the desire to be, or insistence that one is, of the opposite sex. The diagnostic criteria require strong evidence of this desire to be of the opposite sex. Repeated repudiation of the given anatomical sexual structures is accepted as evidence if onset is prior to puberty.

Age of onset is often early; for example, in males, 75% of reported cases began cross-dressing before age four; however, the disorder rarely

TABLE 38
Gender Identity Disorders: DSM-III-R Axis I Codes

302.60	Gender Identity Disorder of Childhood
302.50	Transsexualism
	Specify sexual history
302.85	Gender Identity Disorder of Adolescence or Adulthood, Nontranssexual Type
302.85	Gender Identity Disorder NOS

presents in mental health clinics until the child reaches puberty. Exposure to social conflict often results in repression of the behaviors during late childhood. There is an undetermined association with homosexual patterns in adolescence or later adult life; a relatively infrequent association with transsexualism has also been seen. Occurrence of any other major disorder is rare, though there may be phobias or persistent nightmares. Social impairment varies in relation to the degree of reaction by family and peers.

Transsexualism
Transsexualism is a postpubertal version of Gender Identity Disorder of Childhood. Sexual orientation should be specified (Asexual, Homosexual, Heterosexual, or Unspecified).

Gender Identity Disorder of Adolescence or Adulthood, Nontranssexual Type
This group, like Transsexualism, involves persistent or recurrent discomfort about assigned sex, and cross-dressing in the role of the other sex is usually the major symptom. This disorder differs from Transsexualism in that there is no preoccupation with getting rid of one's primary and secondary sex characteristics, and sexual excitement is not the goal of cross-dressing. The sexual orientation should be specified. This group is particularly interesting as there may be a "compulsive" subgroup of subjects here for whom the cross-dressing has a different basis than for transsexuals.

Gender Identity Disorder Not Otherwise Specified
This category is useful for children or adults with only partial features of the preceding syndromes in terms of either severity or duration.

CASE HISTORIES

Sally
Six-year-old Sally was referred by her kindergarten teacher to the local child guidance clinic because she would not speak during school. She had initially been very tearful and reluctant to have her mother leave her alone in school. Sally's mother said she had been periodically "obstinate" at home but without major problems. After a few weeks, however, she

seemed to become accustomed to the school routine but gradually stopped talking. It was clear from the initial contact and from her nonverbal co-operation that her comprehension and speech development were at age level.

During the beginning of school, the patient's parents separated and the mother became depressed. Home life was physically comfortable and calm, but both parents were rather uninvolved with the patient and with her younger sister. It was hard to find out if there had been much change in speech at home, but the younger sister reported that the patient still spoke with her.

Diagnosis

Axis I:	313.23 Elective Mutism
Axis II:	V71.09 No diagnosis on Axis II
Axis III:	None
Axis IV:	Severity: 3—Moderate (Predominantly enduring circumstances)
	Stressor(s): Parental separation, parental uninvolvement, mother depressed
Axis V:	Current GAF: 60
	Highest GAF past year: 80

Discussion

This patient is typical of Elective Mutism, in that, in spite of the disturbed home situation, no other diagnosable mental disorder is apparent. The extent of true mutism at home is hard to ascertain, but the continuation of speech with at least a sibling is typical.

Charles

Charles, a 14-year-old boy whose parents had been divorced since he was eight, was evaluated because in the past two months he had been breaking a variety of school rules and fighting with other children, quite unlike his previous behavior. This had started after his return from summer vacation. Charles has always had difficulty with reading and is in a special reading program in his junior high school.

He had been in California with his father for the summer. Unlike previous summers, which had been mutually enjoyable, this year his father's time had been monopolized by a girlfriend whom the father planned to marry. She resented Charles's presence and arranged for him to be with children he did not know so she could spend time with the father alone. Charles's mother was upset because the father was trying to reduce child support in connection with his forthcoming marriage.

When interviewed, the boy was friendly toward the examiner, but brash in criticizing the school rules and pointing out what "saps" his friends were. His boasts of being "cool" were out of proportion to any of his true offenses. He said he didn't think he wanted to continue school, but was very receptive to the interviewer's interest in and concern about his future. Psychological testing indicates bright normal intelligence, but reading is two years below grade level.

Diagnosis

Axis I: 309.30 Adjustment Disorder with Disturbance of Conduct
Axis II: 315.00 Developmental Reading Disorder
Axis III: None
Axis IV: Severity: 3—Moderate (Acute event)
            Stressor(s): Loss of nuclear family
Axis V: Current GAF: 70
            Highest GAF past year: 80

Discussion

This boy does not have sufficiently disturbed behavior to meet criteria for Conduct Disorder nor has the disturbance been present very long. His maladaptive behavior, beginning after his visit in the summer, makes a diagnosis of an Adjustment Disorder more appropriate than a V Code. In this case, identifying the stressor on Axis IV is also appropriate and most informative.

Richard

Richard, aged 15, and his mother came to the clinic because of his "compulsion" to dress up as a girl several times each week. He took great pains to do this secretly and would walk around in his female attire in sections of the city where he would not meet anyone he knew. According to both Richard and his mother, he had otherwise normal male behaviors and friendship patterns and denied sexual excitation from these episodes. Their motivation for the consultation was his recent election to a city-wide student council that made recognition in other neighborhoods more likely. On interview, Richard appeared eager to find a way to stop his cross-dressing, claiming great humiliation if he should be found out. His relationship with his family appeared generally supportive.

Diagnosis

Axis I:	302.85 Gender Identity Disorder Not Otherwise Specified
Axis II:	V71.09 No diagnosis on Axis II
Axis III:	None
Axis IV:	Severity: 1—None
	Stressor: N/A
Axis V:	Current GAF: 80
	Highest GAF past year: 80

Discussion

Clearly Richard does not meet criteria for Transsexualism or for Gender Identity Disorder of Adolescence or Adulthood, Nontranssexual Type because of his lack of general discomfort over his assigned sex, as well as his lack of sexual excitement with cross-dressing.

Chapter 16

Use of V Codes

DSM-III adapted from ICD-9-CM (International Classification of Diseases — Clinical Modification) a partial list of conditions that are the focus of clinical attention but are not attributable to mental disorder. In DSM-III-R they are modified only slightly. V Codes indicate that although the condition does not fit the DSM-III definition of "mental disorder," it is serious enough to merit attention and treatment. V Codes may also indicate absence of mental disorder or inadequate evaluation for determination of presence or absence of disorder. Note that they may be coded in *addition* to another Axis I disorder if they are a focus of clinical attention. V Codes may eventually be replaced by a more adequate restructuring of Axis IV (psychosocial stressors). For child psychiatry the specific features found in V Codes may be extremely important for treatment even when an Axis I disorder is present.

Because so many of the V Codes are particularly relevant to clinical work with children and families, clinicians should be aware of their existence and make an effort to use them when applicable. This is, of course, especially appropriate for the instances in which a family or parent problem is the true focus of a child's presenting complaint rather than a disorder within the child.

There may be some redundancy when V Codes and Axis IV factors are both coded; however, V Codes are used on Axis I when the presence of the condition is the cause for contact with the diagnosing agency, is a focus of treatment or attention not attributable to a mental disorder, or thorough evaluation fails to reveal a mental disorder. Axis IV is used to

159

TABLE 39
V Codes: DSM-III-R Axis I and Axis II Codes

Axis I

V62.30	Academic Problem
V71.01	Adult Antisocial Behavior
V71.02	Childhood or Adolescent Antisocial Behavior
V65.20	Malingering
V61.10	Marital Problem
V15.81	Noncompliance with Medical Treatment
V62.20	Occupational Problem
V61.20	Parent-Child Problem
V62.81	Other Interpersonal Problem
V61.80	Other Specified Family Circumstances
V62.89	Phase of Life Problem or Other Life Circumstance Problem
V62.82	Uncomplicated Bereavement
V71.09	No Diagnosis or Condition on Axis I

Axis II

V40.00	Borderline Intellectual Functioning
V71.09	No Diagnosis or Condition on Axis II

provide additional information when a disorder is present and, as it now stands, stresses severity rather than the specific stressors. V Codes currently indicate the presence of a condition requiring treatment in the absence of any other relevant Axis I disorder but can be coded together with an Axis I disorder.

Academic Problem
There is a pattern of failing grades or significant underachievement in the absence of Specific Developmental Disorder or other mental disorder.

Child or Adolescent Antisocial Behavior
This is used for isolated antisocial acts, not apparently due to another disorder such as Conduct Disorder or Adjustment Disorder with Disturbance of Conduct. Such acts often call attention to current family stress.

Marital Problem
Marital conflict related to divorce, estrangement, or separation custody disputes can cause distress for a child otherwise without mental disorder. The primary disturbance would not be attributable to the child being

evaluated, but to his/her circumstances. The marital difficulty is not due to mental disorder on the part of those involved. Alternately, other specified family circumstances could be coded.

Parent-Child Problem

This category can be used when focus of attention is a Parent-Child Problem not due to another apparent mental disorder. An example is child abuse, not attributable to mental disorder in the parent.

Other Specified Family Circumstances

Examples are difficulties with an aged relative or sibling rivalry.

Borderline Intellectual Functioning

This diagnosis is noted on Axis II when the focus of attention or treatment is associated with Borderline Intellectual Functioning (i.e., IQ between 71 and 84). The diagnosis of Borderline Intellectual Functioning is particularly problematic for children in the presence of social and educational deprivation. However, there are many school consultations which arise simply because of the discrepancy between the intellectual level of the child and the surrounding demands of family or of certain school systems. Here this code might be useful even when an Axis I disorder is present.

No Diagnosis

This can be placed on either Axis I or Axis II.

CASE HISTORY

Matthew

Seven-year-old Matthew was brought to the clinic by his stepfather, who complained that he is "too effeminate" and that there "must be something wrong with him." The stepfather was upset, believing that the boy is too "mild" and shows no interest in sports. The mother feels there is nothing wrong with her son, but thinks the stepfather is envious of her close relationship with Matthew and disappointed that they have had no children together. On interview, the boy is somewhat shy, prefers quiet play, but has no other difficulties. Temperamentally, he resembles both his mother and his biological father. His teacher says he functions well in school.

Diagnosis

Axis I:	V61.80 Other Specified Family Circumstances
	V61.20 Parent-Child Problem
Axis II:	V71.09 No diagnosis on Axis II
Axis III:	None
Axis IV:	Axis IV: Severity: 4—Moderate (Acute event)
	Stressor(s): Rejection by stepfather
Axis V:	Current GAF: 85
	Highest GAF past year: 85

Discussion

This could be coded under Parent-Child Problem (V61.20) or Other Specified Family Circumstances (V61.80). Such coding provides a record of the contact and of a problem that is the focus of clinical attention, but does not attribute a mental disorder to the child when in fact none has been determined.

Chapter 17

Specific
Developmental Disorders

The multiaxial approach of DSM-III-R makes it possible to describe disturbance and accompanying features of disorder more completely than any other approach to date. These Axis II disorders delineate specific or otherwise noted deviations from usual development associated with learning and language that are not attributed to another mental disorder. That these difficulties are included within a classification of mental disorders has raised some eyebrows. Objections usually center on the facts that psychopathology is not involved, that diagnostic and treatment functions are usually performed within the educational system, and that such children are stigmatized by inclusion in this classification. Despite these unresolved issues, many instances of Specific Developmental Disorder that require treatment have been cited along with some of the Axis I disorders. Coding of the Axis II disorders in the future will ensure that they are not neglected and may shed some light on their interesting partnership with other disorders (e.g., Attention-Deficit Hyperactivity Disorder and Conduct Disorders). It is also important to note that in many cases Specific Developmental Disorders will be coded on Axis II, while the Axis I code is No Axis I Psychiatric Disorder (V71.09).

Because of their common occurrence, Specific Developmental Disorders should routinely be considered as part of diagnostic differentiation in all cases of developmental delay, school failure, and behavior problems in school or elsewhere. Exact specifications for "significant" delay and detection of Specific Developmental Disorder vary with age of the child. These disorders are not simply deficits in biological maturation; in fact, in most cases, evidence of the difficulty continues into adulthood. In rare cases, symptoms may show improvement over time; however, clinically significant symptoms in adolescence or adulthood should continue to be noted.

EVALUATION AND DIFFERENTIATION

The major diagnostic groups that are differentiated in all cases are Mental Retardation, visual and auditory sensory impairments, and Pervasive Developmental Disorders. Occasionally, in instances of Mild to Moderate Mental Retardation or Pervasive Developmental Disorder, a Specific Developmental Disorder can coexist; that is, developmental impairment may be apparent when compared to other capabilities. This determination requires careful testing and evaluation and familiarity with achievement levels within the retarded range. All diagnoses in this category rely heavily on the results of intellectual, speech, and auditory testing.

DSM-III-R is relatively clear about the criteria for these disorders, and they will not be repeated here. One flaw is that significant degree of disorder is not spelled out nor is any consideration given to age variation in degree of developmental lag. It is important to realize, therefore, the significance that clinical experience plays in accurately recognizing manifestations of these difficulties since there is lack of standardization in determining the definition of deviance. For example, if grade level is used to determine degree of impairment, should achievement be one or two years behind grade level? This criterion would not be too helpful for preschool and early elementary years, a period in which diagnosis and remediation may have a crucial impact on future outcome. Similarly, correction for IQ is important, particularly for children with low-normal intelligence and for those in affluent educational school systems.

There are several more categories in DSM-III-R. Articulation Disorder has been purposely separated from the Language and Speech Disorders, Receptive and Expressive subtypes of Language Disorder have been distinguished, though fifth-digit coding is not available. Expressive Writing Disorder is added as an Academic Skill Disorder and Coordination Disorder, long overdue, has been added.

Some inconsistencies in DSM-III-R's treatment of Specific Developmental Disorders should be pointed out. Most confusing is the inconsistent placement of some disorders on Axis I. While most Specific Developmental Disorders are coded on Axis II, both Stuttering and Clutter-

TABLE 40
Specific Developmental Disorders: DSM-III-R Axis II Codes

Academic Skills Disorders
315.00   Developmental Reading Disorder
315.10   Developmental Arithmetic Disorder
315.80   Developmental Expressive Writing Disorder

Language and Speech Disorders
315.31*   Developmental Expressive Language Disorder
315.31*   Developmental Receptive Language Disorder
315.39   Developmental Articulation Disorder

Motor Skills Disorders
315.40   Developmental Coordination Disorder
315.90*   Specific Developmental Disorder Not Otherwise Specified
315.90*   Developmental Disorder Not Otherwise Specified

*Used for more than one DSM-III-R code in order to maintain compatibility with ICD-9-CM.

ing are coded on Axis I (see Chapter 15). Elimination disorders, Functional Enuresis and Encopresis, were kept on Axis I in part because of the difficulty in categorizing as a Developmental Disorder an ability that has been achieved and then is lost (i.e., the *Secondary* vs. *Primary* distinction). However, the pattern of association with development and the usually early onset make them seem more appropriate for Axis II.

A welcome addition to DSM-III-R is Developmental Coordination Disorder (the clumsy child syndrome). Although children described as "clumsy" do not form a homogeneous group (Henderson, 1987), lack of motor coordination has had a long association with a variety of forms of psychopathology, including Attention-Deficit Hyperactivity and Anxiety Disorders (Shaffer et al., 1978). Its inclusion on Axis II is long overdue. Problems still remain for defining clumsy behaviors. DSM-III-R requires coordination to be markedly below expected developmental level, to the degree that it significantly interferes with academic or daily accomplishments. However, most diagnostic tests for motor abilities do not tap the lack of abilities indicated here, and separate assessments of motor skills correlate poorly with one another. In addition, systematic data have yet to be collected on the treatment of Developmental Coordination Disorder. The usefulness of this diagnosis will be to better understand a child's handicaps, to study associated patterns of disturbance, and ultimately to discover the prognostic significance of developmental clumsiness per se.

CASE HISTORY

Carl

Carl, seven years old, is brought to the clinic at the request of his school psychologist because of difficulty with schoolwork and restless behavior in class. Carl is seen as immature and often does not appear to listen when the teacher gives instructions. He has always had poor coordination.

The parents, both high-school graduates, have had no complaints about Carl up to this time, although the mother thinks Carl was somewhat slow in starting to talk and to speak in full sentences.

Examination in the clinic shows a friendly, cooperative child who is mildly restless during the examination. Psycholinguistic testing indicates immature language development in spite of good ability to understand instructions. Carl's spoken language is clear but immature, and he uses relatively simple and concrete phrases. Reading ability is also below age level. Full Scale IQ is 90; Verbal 80; Performance 105.

Diagnosis

Axis I:	Attention-Deficit Hyperactivity Disorder (Mild); (Provisional)
Axis II:	315.31 Developmental Expressive Language Disorder
Axis III:	None
Axis IV:	Severity: 0 — Inadequate information Stressor(s): N/A
Axis V:	Current GAF: 75 Highest GAF past year: 80

Discussion

Without psychological testing, Carl could be misdiagnosed as a "simple case" of Attention-Deficit Hyperactivity Disorder. The more important remediation here is educational and psycholinguistic. Moreover, without attention to the differential diagnosis of a reading difficulty, the basis for the reading problem would go undetected. A diagnosis of Developmental Reading Disorder is premature in this case.

Epidemiological data show a powerful association between the Developmental Language Disorders and a variety of Axis I syndromes (Cantwell & Baker, 1985). Carl's case is typical, as at least half of the children with Developmental Language Disorders exhibit some behavioral disturbance. The mechanisms mediating this relationship are not understood.

Chapter 18

Conclusions

DSM-III-R seems clear in its criteria and in its descriptive, atheoretical approach. This may lead to a false sense of security in practicing diagnostics. The most difficult part of the diagnostic process is recognizing the specific behaviors and the degree of impairment they may represent. Usually, an extensive combination of clinical training and experience is required to attain the degree of expertise needed to apply a diagnostic system. Intensive exposure to children with specific handicaps and specific behavioral disturbances at all ages—from infancy to early adulthood for childhood disorders—is essential for mastery of diagnosis.

At a board examination for child psychiatry several years ago, one of the authors was struck by the frequency with which an "exam case," a videotape of a five-year-old deaf child, was diagnosed as *autistic*. The examinees knew the "DSM criteria" for autism perfectly; however, they incorrectly evaluated the behaviors of the child shown on the videotape, interpreting dance steps as "abnormal stereotyped movements" and sign language between child and teacher simply as the "absence of speech" associated with autism. Improved clarity within the diagnostic classification system cannot address this kind of ignorance.

Development of diagnostic sense in child psychiatry and other disciplines requires hundreds of hours of supervised exposure to normal and abnormal children with a wide variety of symptom patterns. It is beyond the scope of this book to outline clinical training for child psychiatry, except to stress the desirability of supervision in which senior supervisors also have direct contact with the case through tapes, sitting in on or observing the interview, or through an additional independent interview. Clear descriptive labels are actually the second step in the success of DSM-III-R. The first step must be to know what you are seeing.

ON TO DSM-IV

The DSM is continually under reexamination and revision. DSM-III-R is just a preliminary version on the path to DSM-IV. A task force has been assembled by the American Psychiatric Association to make recommendations for DSM-IV. Information from the "consumers" balanced with research evidence will, in fact, be the making of DSM-IV.

Relationship to ICD-10

Ideally, research studies and validating replications should be the basis for the changes. With the small research force within child psychiatry, the changes are likely to be small. A major issue facing the new APA task force will be the need to remain as compatible as possible with ICD-10, the official classificatory scheme of the World Health Organization which is in almost final form, subject only to some last minute tinkering, and will be adopted by the World Health Assembly in 1990. This latest draft of the international classification system has been heavily influenced by DSM-III. But major differences remain between DSM-III-R and the proposed ICD-10 which (except for its use in England) is not multiaxial (see Appendix I).

Validity of Axis I Disorders and Multiplicity of Diagnoses

We see an important agenda for DSM-III-R within child psychiatry. This encompasses validation of several Axis I entities and probable alteration of some of those now on Axis II as well. Since DSM-III-R urges multiple diagnoses, clinicians are likely to list more individual diagnoses per patient. This is where the work comes in—making sense of these tabulations. Critics are concerned that this approach has already gotten out of hand; however, future DSM task forces will have to consider the relative merits of multiple diagnoses, compared with differential diagnosis, in the areas where validity of the distinctions is, as yet, unproven. Perhaps most important, a coding scheme for cases to tabulate degree of association of diagnoses needs to be devised, as at present such accounting is carried out satisfactorily only at research centers.

Axis I probably has more disorders than it should. For example, it is not clear whether the split between Overanxious Disorder of Childhood or Adolescence and Anxiety Disorder for adults is justified. DSM-III-R has reduced the subtypes of Conduct and Attention-Deficit Hyperactivity Disorders, but the status of Oppositional Defiant Disorder still has to be clarified. Is it a precursor to other disorders—Major Depression, Conduct Disorder, Personality Disorders—to one, or to or all of them? As now defined, it is less likely to be a normal phase and more likely to be a disorder in its own right, but which kind? The application and appropriateness of DSM-III-R categories in the preschool age also deserve a great deal more attention and data.

Use of Axes II, IV, and V for Childhood Diagnosis
The shift of Mental Retardation and Pervasive Developmental Disorders to Axis II in DSM-III-R is an improvement over their placement on Axis I. A remaining reservation about this change is that having both Mental Retardation and Pervasive Developmental Disorder on the same axis might lead to one or the other being overlooked. The possibility of placing Mental Retardation on a separate axis was carefully considered, but the prevailing wisdom was to resist adding more axes.

For children and adolescents, some personality disturbances can be coded on Axis I. Diagnosing Personality Disorders is confusing in any case, certainly in this age group. Only now are reliable structured instruments gaining wider use for diagnosis of Personality Disorders. Since Borderline and Narcissistic Personality Disorders are becoming more frequently diagnosed in adolescents, standardization of these instruments should include this age group. Research is also needed in order to determine relationships and common features and characteristics that occur in Identity Disorder and in adults with Borderline Personality Disorder.

The most substantial critiques of the multiaxial structure of DSM have focused on Axis IV. In DSM-III-R both the severity and specific type of stressor are now coded. DSM-III-R states that stressors should be coded if they may have contributed to the onset of or worsening of the disorder. Axis IV could and should have prognostic value and be important for management planning and for clinical research. In theory, the descriptive focus of Axes I and II, combined with the ratings of psychosocial stressors, could facilitate research. For example, one could examine specific stressors in relation to particular disorders. In practice, the existing Axis IV does not incorporate available empirical research. For example, parental divorce is listed as an acute event even though clinical and research data argue against this (Wallerstein, 1983).

Axis V, the current level of adaptive functioning and the highest level in the past year, also has pitfalls particularly for children. If the illness has lasted more than a year, the second rating may be deceptively low. Even experienced clinicians show low reliability on Axes IV and V ratings unless there is extensive training in their use (Cantwell, 1988; Prendergast et al., 1988; van Goor-Lambo, 1987).

Once again we extend a cautionary note concerning the clinical application of the diagnostic system. Use of DSM-III-R can only reflect the clinician's ability to correctly identify patient symptoms. Awareness of the differing limitations in collecting useful data extends beyond the hindrances of the classification system to the degree of error in recognizing behaviors. DSM-III-R is not a surrogate for experience; however, in proper hands it will be a powerful aid in the advancement of knowledge.

The opportunity for systematic observation and clear documentation and communication should prove useful to the private practitioner interested in collecting data for follow-up assessment in relation to treatment or naturalistic course. Commentary on the diagnostic gray areas in light of this kind of meticulous application will expedite future revisions and provide invaluable input for diagnostic understanding of childhood disorders.

DSM-III-R and ICD-10 (1988 Draft) for Disorders First Arising in Childhood or Adolescence

DSM-III received criticism from abroad because of its departure from the structure of ICD-9, and from the nomenclature developed by the World Health Organization (WHO) for classification of disease. It should be noted that ICD (International Classification of Disease) terminology is also acceptable to most U.S. hospitals and third-party providers. As this guide goes to press, ICD-10 is almost in final form and is likely to be approved for publication by WHO in 1990 with implementation following by 1993. In general DSM-III-R and ICD-10 are more similar than their predecessors, DSM-III and ICD-9, because of concerted effort by WHO and the Alcohol, Drug Abuse and Mental Health Administration (ADAMHA) to improve international psychiatric exchange.

There are several differences between the draft of ICD-9 and ICD-10. The number of categories for mental disorders has increased (from 30 to 100); in childhood disorders this is particularly noticeable in the area of Developmental Disorders.

Somewhat confusingly, there are actually three versions of ICD-10. There is a shorter, official version; a longer, "blue book" version; and a not yet complete version containing research diagnostic criteria.

The most recent version of ICD-10 was altered in many different ways to be more in line with DSM-III-R. For example, Oppositional Defiant Disorder is included now in ICD-10, and various subtypes of Overactive Disorder were delineated more clearly to avoid confusion with other causes of childhood overactivity (e.g., see Overactive Disorder Associated with Mental Retardation and Stereotyped Movements).

In several areas (Autism, Hyperactivity, and Conduct Disorder) there are more ICD-10 diagnoses than for DSM-III-R. Extrapolating clinical and research data across nations will have to take these differences into account. For example, ICD-10 breaks down the Pervasive Developmental Disorders more than does DSM-III-R. In ICD-10, both Rett syndrome (Childhood Disintegrative Disorder) and Asperger's syndrome can be coded separately. ICD-10 conceptualizes emotional disorders with childhood onset in part on the basis of developmental appropriateness, whereas DSM-III-R focuses on specific syndromes without such an overarching concept. The subdivisions of Conduct Disorders are unsatisfactory in both classifications (Prendergast et al., 1988). ICD-10 has chosen to retain a different distinction (socialized/unsocialized) than did DSM-III-R (group/solitary-aggressive).

Perhaps most important is a difference in philosophy between the two systems: DSM-III-R, like its predecessor, encourages multiple diagnostic codings whereas ICD-10, while allowing occasional multiple codings, generally discourages this practice. The most important mixed categories in ICD-10, from the standpoint of child psychiatry, are Mixed Disturbance of Conduct and Emotions (F.92) and Hyperkinetic Conduct Disorder (F.90.1). The best argument in favor of retaining the ICD-10 mixed categories is that individual cases with the overlap are identified, whereas with the current tabulation systems for multiple diagnoses, the number of cases with both diagnoses is less likely to be so marked.

Finally, ICD-10 is not multiaxial although a multiaxial version is in use in the United Kingdom. Axis V from that version completes Appendix I, as it is of particular use in pediatric cases.

In order to demonstrate key similarities and differences, Table AI-1 lists DSM-III-R and the corresponding ICD-10 (draft of September 1988) diagnoses that most pertain to children and adolescents. The following is adapted in part from work by Drs. Michael First and Robert Spitzer. In many cases, it is not simple to go from DSM-III-R to ICD-10 because either there is no exact "translation" or there are several to choose from, depending on the particular patient's symptoms. In some cases, there is no comparable diagnosis. Nevertheless, both systems are much closer now.

TABLE AI-1
Comparison of DSM-III-R and ICD-10 (1988 Draft)

DSM-III-R		ICD-10 (Draft, Sept. 1988)	
Mental Retardation			
317.00	Mild Mental Retardation	F70.9	Mild Mental Retardation
318.00	Moderate Mental Retardation	F71.9	Moderate Mental Retardation
318.10	Severe Mental Retardation	F72.9	Severe Mental Retardation
318.20	Profound Mental Retardation	F73.9	Profound Mental Retardation
319.00	Unspecified Mental Retardation	F79.9	Unspecified Mental Retardation
Pervasive Developmental Disorders			
299.00	Autistic Disorder	F84.0	Childhood Autism
		F84.1	Atypical Autism
299.80	Pervasive Developmental Disorder DOS	F84.2	Childhood Disintegrative Disorder
		F84.3	Overactive Disorder Associated with Stereotyped Movements
		F84.4	Schizoid Disorder of Childhood
		F84.8	Other
		F84.9	Unspecified
Specific Developmental Disorders			
Academic Skills Disorders			
315.10	Developmental Arithmetic Disorder	F81.2	Specific Disorder of Arithmetic Skills
315.80	Developmental Expressive Writing Disorder	F81.9	Other and Unspecified Disorders of Scholastic Skills
315.00	Developmental Reading Disorder	F81.0	Specific Reading Disorder
Language and Speech Disorders			
315.39	Developmental Articulation Disorder	F80.0	Simple Speech Articulation Disorder
315.31	Developmental Expressive Language Disorder	F80.1	Expressive Language Disorder
315.31	Developmental Receptive Language Disorder	F80.2	Receptive Language Disorder

(continued)

TABLE AI-1 (continued)

DSM-III-R		ICD-10 (Draft, Sept. 1988)	
	Motor Skills Disorder		
315.40	Developmental Coordination Disorder	F82	Specific Developmental Disorder of Motor Function
315.90	Specific Developmental Disorder NOS	F81.1	Specific Spelling Disorder
		F81.3	Mixed Disorder of Scholastic Skills
		F81.8	Other Specific Developmental Disorder of Scholastic Skills
		F81.9	Developmental Disorder of Scholastic Skill Unspecified
		F80.3	Environmentally Determined Language Disorder
		F80.4	Acquired Aphasia with Epilepsy
		F80.8	Other Specific Developmental Disorder of Speech and Language
Speech Disorders Not Elsewhere Classified			
307.00	Cluttering	F98.7	Cluttering
307.00	Stuttering	F98.6	Stuttering (stammering)
Disruptive Behavior Disorders			
314.01	Attention-Deficit Hyperactivity Disorder	F90	Hyperkinetic Disorder
		F90.0	Simple Disturbance of Activity and Attention
		F90.1	Hyperkinetic Conduct Disorder
		F90.8	Other
		F90.9	Unspecified
312.20	Conduct Disorder, Group Type	F91	Conduct Disorder
312.00	Conduct Disorder, Solitary Aggressive Type	F91.0	Conduct Disorder Confined to the Family Context
312.90	Conduct Disorder, Undifferentiated Type	F91.1	Unsocialized Conduct Disorder
		F91.2	Socialized Conduct Disorder
313.81	Oppositional Defiant Disorder	F91.8	Other Conduct Disorder

Anxiety Disorders of Childhood or Adolescence

309.21	Separation Anxiety Disorder	F93.0	Separation Anxiety Disorder
313.21	Avoidant Disorder of Childhood or Adolescence	F93.2	Social Sensitivity Disorder
		F40.1	Social Phobias
		F93.8	Other Emotional Disorder (with Onset Specific to Childhood)
313.00	Overanxious Disorder	F93.1	Phobic Disorder of Childhood
		F41.1	Generalized Anxiety Disorder
		F93.8	Other Emotional Disorder (with Onset Specific to Childhood)

Oppositional Defiant Disorder

F91.9	Unspecified
F92	Mixed Disorder of Conduct and Emotions
F92.0	Depressive Conduct Disorder
F92.8	Other
F92.9	Unspecified

Eating Disorders

307.10	Anorexia Nervosa	F50.0	Anorexia Nervosa
307.51	Bulimia Nervosa	F50.1	Bulimia Nervosa
		F50.2	Normal Weight Bulimia
307.52	Pica	F98.3	Pica
307.53	Rumination Disorder of Infancy	F98.2	Eating Disorder (Other Than Pica) in Infancy and Childhood

Gender Identity Disorders

302.60	Gender Identity Disorder of Childhood	F64.8	Other Gender Identity Disorder
302.50	Transsexualism	F64.0	Transsexualism
302.85	Gender Identity Disorder of Adolescence or Adulthood, Nontranssexual type	F64.1	Dual Role Transvestism
302.85	Gender Identity Disorder NOS	F64.8	Other Gender Identity Disorder
		F64.9	Gender Identity Disorder, Unspecified

(continued)

175

TABLE AI-1 (continued)

DSM-III-R		ICD-10 (Draft, Sept. 1988)	
Tic Disorders			
307.23	Tourette's Disorder	F95.2	Combined Vocal and Multiple Motor Tics (Tourette Syndrome)
307.22	Chronic Motor or Vocal Tic	F95.1	Chronic Motor or Vocal Tic Disorder
307.21	Transient Tic Disorder	F95.0	Transient Tic Disorder
307.20	Tic Disorder NOS	F95.8	Other Tic Disorder
		F95.9	Tic Disorder, Unspecified
Disorders of Elimination			
307.70	Functional Encopresis	F98.1	Encopresis
307.60	Functional Enuresis	F98.0	Enuresis
Other Disorders of Infancy, Childhood, or Adolescence			
313.23	Elective Mutism	F94.0	Elective Mutism
313.82	Identity Disorder	F93.8	Other Emotional Disorder (with Onset Specific to Childhood)
313.89	Reactive Attachment Disorder of Infancy or Early Childhood	F94.1	Reactive Attachment Disorder of Childhood
		F94.2	Attachment Disorder of Childhood, Disinhibition Type
307.30	Stereotypy/Habit Disorder	F98.5	Stereotype Movement Disorder
314.00	Undifferentiated Attention-Deficit Disorder	F99	Mental Disorder, Unspecified

176

ICD/U.K. AXIS V: Associated Abnormal Psychosocial Situations

The ICD/U.K. Axis V was prepared by Rutter, Shaffer, and Shepherd (1975). We include it here because of the significance of psychosocial situations in child and adolescent psychiatry. However, we acknowledge that its use is still problematic since satisfactory reliability has yet to be demonstrated for several categories, although some modification may resolve this issue (van Goor-Lambo, 1987).

Principles

This axis concerns aspects of the patient's current psychosocial situation which are markedly abnormal in the context of the patient's level of development and sociocultural circumstances. Situations should be coded irrespective of whether they are thought to have directly caused psychiatric disorder. However, situations that are abnormal solely as part of the patient's symptomatology should be excluded.

TABLE AI-2
ICD/U.K. Axis V: Associated Abnormal Psychosocial Situations*

More than one coding may be made on this axis. If this is done, codings should be put in order of importance with respect to the patient.

01.   Mental Disturbance in Other Family Members
Includes: any kind of overt, handicapping psychiatric disorder or any kind of gross abnormality of behavior (not necessarily receiving psychiatric treatment) in a member of the patient's immediate household or in a parent or sibling.
Excludes: mental retardation in a family member if this is unassociated with behavioral abnormality. Psychiatric disorder in more distant relatives if they are not in the same household.

02.   Discordant Intrafamilial Relationships
Includes: discord or disharmony (such as shown by hostility, quarreling, scapegoating, etc.) of sufficient severity to lead to a persisting atmosphere in the home or to persisting interpersonal tensions. Discordant relationships between the two parents, discordant relationships between parent and patient, and discordant relationships with a sibling should be included here (irrespective of whether they are living together).
Excludes: lack of warmth or affection (03) if not associated with discord.

(continued)

---

*From *A Guide to a Multi-Axial Classification Scheme for Psychiatric Disorders—Childhood and Adolescence.* Prepared by M. L. Rutter, D. Shaffer, and C. Sturge. Department of Child and Adolescent Psychiatry, Institute of Psychiatry, DeCrespigny Park, London SE5 A8AF, England.

TABLE AI-2 *(continued)*

03. **Lack of Warmth in Intrafamilial Relationships**
Includes: a *marked* lack of warmth or affection; or a coldness and distance in the relationships between the parents or between parent and patient (irrespective of whether they are living together); lack of empathetic responsiveness as distinct from punitiveness or restrictiveness.
Excludes: discord and disharmony (02) if in the context of warm relationships.

04. **Familial Overinvolvement**
Includes: a *marked* excess of intrusiveness (such as shown by overprotection, overrestriction, incestuous relationships, or undue emotional stimulation, etc.) by another family member when judged in relation to the patient's maturity level and the sociofamilial context.
Excludes: increased control which is appropriate to the patient's developmental level and behavior.

05. **Inadequate or Inconsistent Parental Control**
Includes: a *marked* lack of effective control or supervision of the patient's activities when judged in relation to the patient's maturity level and the sociofamilial context.
Markedly inconsistent or inefficient discipline should be coded here.

06. **Inadequate Social, Linguistic, or Perceptual Stimulation**
Includes: a *marked* lack of effective and meaningful social, linguistic, *or* perceptual experiences when judged in relation to the patient's developmental needs; whether arising as a result of inadequate or inappropriate parent-child interaction, periods of poor quality substitute care, or for any other reason. A marked lack of toys, a failure to engage the child in adequate play or conversation, or a gross isolation from other children would be included. An institutional upbringing which provided adequate cognitive stimulation but a marked lack of affective ties should also be coded here.

07. **Inadequate Living Conditions**
Includes: *grossly* inadequate living conditions, however caused. Marked poverty, lack of basic household amenities (bath, hot running water, etc.), overcrowding (to the extent of at least 1-5 persons per all rooms used for living, dining, or sleeping), shared beds, vermin infestation of home, and severe damp would all be included.

08. **Inadequate or Distorted Intrafamilial Communication**
Includes: a *marked* lack or distortion of communication or discussion between family members of such severity that important family issues are either not discussed or are the subject of misleading messages between family members.

TABLE AI-2 *(continued)*

Excludes: quarrelsome interchanges which nevertheless allow adequate discussion of important issues even if negative feelings prevent their resolution (02).

09. Anomalous Family Situation
Includes: an institutional environment (other than that arising from a limited episode of hospital care), single parent family, upbringing by a homosexual couple, fostering, or multiple parenting when there is no immediate family context.
Excludes: *past* separations or break-up of the family unless associated with a currently anomalous family situation; upbringing by a married couple one or both of whom are not biologically related to the child; communal upbringing when there is also a family group.

10. Stresses or Disturbances in School or Work Environment
Includes: any *marked* acute or chronic stress or disturbance in the person's school or work environment such as that caused by severe interpersonal tensions, bullying, isolation from peers, inability to cope with the work involved, personal loss, or marked instability in the school or work environment.
Excludes: disturbances which are solely part of the patient's disorder.

11. Migration or Social Transplantation
Includes: recent migration or movement of the patient to a different sociocultural environment or any kind of move which results in a severe disruption of personal ties or relationships (such as eviction resulting in break-up of the family or homelessness).

12. Natural Disaster
Includes: any recent disaster impinging on the patient which arises as a result of natural causes which leads to severe social disruption or social disadvantage. Floods, earthquakes, volcanos, landslides, damage due to storm would all be included.
Excludes: disasters due to war, riot, or accident (16).

13. Other Intrafamilial Psychosocial Stress
Includes: any recent or current *marked* stress on the patient arising within the family such as caused by bereavement, divorce, or separation; illness, accident, or physical handicap of a member of the patient's immediate family; or the departure of a loved person from within the home.
Excludes: acute stresses arising outside the family such as caused by the death of a friend (14) or stresses at school/work (10).

(continued)

TABLE AI-2 *(continued)*

14.   Other Extrafamilial Psychosocial Stress
Includes: any recent or current *marked* stress on the patient arising outside
the family such as caused by bereavement, illness, accident, broken
important relationship, personal rejection, or personal failure.
Excludes: acute stresses arising within the family (13), stresses in the school or
work environment (10).

15.   Persecutiorror Adverse Discrimination
Includes: any kind of persecution or gross adverse discrimination on the basis
of racial, social, religious, or other group characteristics which
directly impinges on the patient.
Excludes: bullying or teasing at school or work on the basis of personal
characteristics (10).

16.   Other Psychosocial Disturbance in Society in General
Includes: any chronic psychosocial disturbance in society in general which
directly and markedly impinges on the patient. War, civil unrest,
famine, pandemics, and other persisting disruptions of social life
would be included here.

88.   Other (specified)
Includes: any acute or chronic stress, distortion, or disadvantage in a person's
psychosocial environment which is not codable above.
Excludes: physical disabilities (code under axis 4) intellectual disabilities
(code under axis 3) genetic predisposition (not coded unless
associated with a codeable psychosocial situation on this axis or a
codeable medical, intellectual, or developmental condition on
other axes).

99.   Psychosocial Situation Unknown

Diagnostic Scales and Interviews

There are many interview and behavior rating instruments for children and adolescents in clinical use and for clinical research. Since the first edition of this *Guide*, scales have been developed and improved for a variety of areas. The time-honored ratings for home and classroom hyperactivity have been extended to cover adolescence. Newer scales now cover Mood Disorders and Eating Disorders. In addition, several specialized scales for Pervasive Developmental Disorder and Obsessive Compulsive Disorder reflect the recent treatment research with these conditions.

DIAGNOSTIC SCALES

A special issue of the *Psychopharmacology Bulletin* (Rapoport & Conners, 1985) reviewed these scales and reprinted many of them. A list of the scales available in this issue is given in Table AII-1.

PATIENT INTERVIEWS

The development of pediatric psychiatric interviews has also advanced considerably. Since the pioneering efforts of Rutter and Graham (1968), a variety of instruments, most notably the Children's Assessment Scale (CAS), the Diagnostic Interview for Children and Adolescents (DICA), the NIMH Diagnostic Interview Schedule (DISC), the Interview Schedule for Children (ISC), and the Kiddie SADS, have been further developed, and reliability data are available for all. Table AII-2 summarizes the contents and relative characteristics of each.

TABLE AII-1
Rating Scales of Childhood Psychopathology*

Demographic Data and Family History
Documentation of Demographic Data and Family History
   of Psychiatric Illness
Demographic Template
Research Obstetrical Scale (ROS)

General Behavior Scale
Parent Symptom Questionnaire
Teacher Questionnaire
Teacher Questionnaire (Follow-up School Report)
Inpatient Global Rating Scale (IGRS)
Child Behavior Rating Form
(Child Behavior Profile; Revised Child Behavior Checklist)
Clinical Global Impression (CGI)

Ratings for Eating Disorders
Anorexic Behavior Scale
Anorexic Attitude Questionnaire
Eating Attitudes Test
Eating Disorder Inventory
Binge Scale Questionnaire
Binge-Eating Questionnaire
Bulimia Interview Form
Eating Disorders Questionnaire

Ratings for Autism
Behavioral and Cognitive Measures Used in Psychophar-
   macological Studies of Infantile Autism
Childhood Autism Rating Scale (CARS)

Ratings for Attention Deficit Disorders
ADD-H Comprehensive Teacher's Rating Scale (ACTeRS)
ADD-H Adolescent Self-Report Scale
Parent Questionnaire of Teenage Behavior (Modified Conners)
Self-Evaluation (Teenager's) Self-Report
Adult Questionnaire-Childhood Characteristics (AQCC) Scale

Ratings for Obsessive-Compulsive Disorders
The Leyton Obsessional Inventory-Child Version

Ratings for Anxiety Disorders
Children's Manifest Anxiety Scale: Parent Ratings
Children's Manifest Anxiety Scale: Child Ratings
Parent's Questionnaire (Modified Conners): Anxiety and Mood Items Added
Teacher Rating Scale (Modified Conners): Anxiety and Mood Items Added

Ratings for Childhood Depression
DMS-III Symptom Checklist for Major Depressive Disorders
The Bellevue Index of Depression (BID)
Peer Nomination Index of Depression (PNID)
School Age Depression Listed Inventory (SADLI)
Interview for the SADLI
Children's Depression Rating Scale-Revised
The Children's Depression Inventory (CDI)

*Available in Rapoport & Conners (1985)

TABLE AII-2
Characteristics and Content of Interviews*

Interview Properties	CAS	DICA	DISC	ISC	K-SADS
Number of items	128	267-311	264-302	200+	200+
Time period assessed	Current or past 6 months	Current or ever	Past year	2 weeks or past 6 months	Current or lifetime
Age assessed	7-17	6-17	6-17	8-17	6-17
Completion time	45-60 min	60-90 min	50-70 min	60-90 min	45-120 min
Structured		X	X		
Semistructured	X			X	X
Symptom oriented	X		X	X	
Category oriented		X		X	X
Severity ratings				X	X
Pre-coded	X	X	X	X	X
Computer scoring		X	X		

*The interviews can be obtained from their developers:

184

	Column 1	Column 2	Column 3	Column 4	Column 5
Administration					
Lay interviewer		X	X		
Clinician	X	X	X	X	X
Reliability data	X	X	X	X	X
Axis I Disorders:					
Affective Disorders					
Adjustment Disorders with Depressed Mood				X	
Cyclothymia	X		X		X
Dysthymia	X	X	X	X	X
Hypomania				X	X
Major Depression	X	X	X	X	X
Mania	X	X	X	X	X
Minor Depression					X

(continued)

185

TABLE AII-2 (continued)

Interview Properties	CAS	DICA	DISC	ISC	K-SADS
Anxiety Disorders					
Avoidant	X	X	X	X	
Generalized Anxiety	X				X
Obsessive Compulsive	X	X	X	X	X
Overanxious	X	X	X	X	X
Panic	X		X	X	X
Phobic	X	X	X	X	X
Separation Anxiety	X	X	X	X	X
Behavioral Disorders					
Attention-Deficit	X	X	X	X	X
Conduct	X	X	X	X	X
Oppositional	X	X	X	X	
Eating Disorders					
Anorexia Nervosa	X	X	X		X
Bulimia	X	X	X		X

Children's Assessment Scale (CAS)
Kay Hodges, Ph.D.
University of Missouri School of Medicine
One Hospital Drive
N119 Medical Center
Columbia, Missouri 65212

Diagnostic Interview for Children and Adolescents (DICA)
Zila Welner, M.D., and Wendy Reich, Ph.D.
Washington University School of Medicine
4940 Audubon Avenue
St. Louis, Missouri 63110

Diagnostic Interview Schedule for Children (DISC)
Anthony Costello, M.D.
Department of Psychiatry
University of Massachusetts Medical Center
55 Lake Avenue North
Worcester, Massachusetts 01655

Interview Schedule for Children (ISC)
Marika Kovacs, Ph.D.
Western Psychiatric Institute and Clinic
3811 O'Hara Street
Pittsburgh, Pennsylvania 15213

Kiddie SADS (K-SADS)
Joaquim Puig-Antich, M.D., and
Helen Orvaschel, Ph.D.
Western Psychiatric Institute and Clinic
3811 O'Hara Street
Pittsburgh, Pennsylvania 15213

187

References

Aman, M.: Stimulant drug effects in Developmental Disorders and Hyperactivity—Toward a resolution of disparate findings. *J. Autism Dev. Disorders*, 1982, 12:385–398.

American Psychiatric Association: *Diagnostic and statistical manual of mental disorders* (3rd ed.—revised). Washington, D.C.: American Psychiatric Press, Inc., 1987.

Beardslee, W., Klerman, G., Keller, M., Lavori, P., & Podorefsky, D.: But are they cases? Validity of DSM-III Major Depression in children identified in a family study. *Am. J. Psychiat.*, 1985, 142:687–691.

Bradley, C.: The behavior of children receiving benzedrine. *Am. J. Orthopsychiatry*, 1937, 94:577–585.

Campbell, M., Geller, B., & Cohen, I.: Current status of drug research and treatment with autistic children. *J. Pediatr. Psychol.*, 1977, 2:153–161.

Cantor, S., Evans, J., & Pezzot-Pearce, T.: Childhood Schizophrenia: Present but not accounted for. *Am. J. Psychiat.*, 1982, 139:758–762.

Cantwell, D.: DSM-III studies. In: M. Rutter, A. Tuma, & I. Lann (Eds.), *Assessment and diagnosis in child psychopathology*. New York: Guilford Press, 1988, pp. 3-36.

Cantwell, D., & Baker, L.: Speech and language development and disorders. In: M. Rutter, & M. Herson (Eds.), *Child and adolescent psychiatry: Modern approaches* (2nd ed.). Oxford: Blackwell Scientific Publications, 1985, pp. 526-544.

Cantwell, D., Russell, A., Mattison, R., & Will, L.: A comparison of DSM-II and DSM-III in the diagnosis of childhood psychiatric disorders: I. Agreement with expected diagnosis. *Arch. Gen. Psychiat.*, 1979a, 36:1208–1213.

Cantwell, D., Russell, A., Mattison, R., & Will, L.: A comparison of DSM-II and DSM-III in the diagnosis of childhood psychiatric disorders: IV. Difficulties in use, global comparisons, and conclusions. *Arch. Gen. Psychiat.*, 1979b, 36:1227–1228.

Carlson, G., & Cantwell, D.: Diagnosis of childhood Depression: A comparison of Weinberg and DSM-III criteria. *J. Am. Acad. Child Psychiat.*, 1982a, 21:247–250.

Carlson, G. & Cantwell, D.: A survey of depressive symptoms, syndrome and disorder in a child psychiatric population. *J. Child Psychol. Psychiat.*, 1982b, 21:19–25.

Cohen, D., Paul, R., & Volkmar, F.: Issues in the classification of Pervasive and Other Developmental Disorders: Toward DSM-IV. *J. Am. Acad. Child Psychiat.*, 1986, 25:213–220.

Creak, M.: Schizophrenic syndrome in childhood. *Dev. Med. Child Neurol.*, 1964, 6:530–535.

189

Denckla, M.: Revised physical and neurological examination for soft signs. *Psychopharmacol. Bull.*, 1985, 21:773–793.

Dickerson, S., Humphrey, F., Handford, H., & Mitchell, J.: Rumination Disorder: Differential diagnoses. *J. Am. Acad. Child Psychiat.*, 1988, 27:300–302.

Dyson, L., & Barcai, A.: Treatment of lithium responding patients. *Curr. Ther. Res.*, 1970, 12:286–290.

Earls, T.: Application of DSM-III in an epidemiological study of preschool children. *Am. J. Psychiat.*, 1982, 139:242–243.

Edelbrock, C., Costello, A., Dulcan, M., Conover, N., & Kala, R.: Parent-child agreement on child psychiatric symptoms assessed via structured interview. *J. Child Psychol. Psychiat.*, 1986, 27:181–190.

Eisenberg, L.: When is a case a case? In: M. Rutter, C. Izard, & P. Read (Eds.), *Depression in young people: Developmental and clinical perspectives*. New York: Guilford Press, 1986, pp. 469–478.

Endicott, J., Spitzer, R., Fleiss, J., et al.: The Global Assessment Scale: A procedure for measuring overall severity of psychiatric disturbance. *Arch. Gen. Psychiat.*, 1976, 33:766–771.

Fish, B.: Neurobiologic antecedents of Schizophrenia in children. *Arch. Gen. Psychiat.*, 1977, 37:1297–1313.

Flament, M., Whitaker, A., Rapoport, J., Davies, M., Berg, C., Kalikow, K., Sceery, W., & Shaffer, J.: Obsessive Compulsive Disorder in adolescence: An epidemiological study. *J. Am. Acad. Child Adol. Psychiat.*, 1988, 27:764–771.

Folstein, S. & Rutter, M.: Autism: Familial aggregation and genetic implications. In: E. Schopler & G. Mesibou (Eds.), *Neurobiological issues in Autism*. New York: Plenum Press, 1987, pp. 83–105.

Geller, B., Chestnut, E., Miller, M., Price, D., & Yates, E.: Preliminary data on DSM-III associated features of Major Depressive Disorder in children and adolescents. *Am. J. Psychiat.*, 1985, 142:643–644.

Gittelman, R.: *Anxiety Disorders of childhood*. New York: Guilford Press, 1986.

Gittelman, R.: The role of psychological tests for differential diagnosis in child psychiatry. *J. Am. Acad. Child Psychiat.*, 1980, 19:413–438.

Gittelman, R., & Abikoff, H.: Pure Conduct Disorder and stimulant medication. Paper presented at NIMH workshop on conduct disorder, Bethesda, MD., November 21, 1986.

Gittelman, R., Manuzza, S., Shenker, R., & Bonagura, N.: Hyperactive boys almost grown up. I. Psychiatric status. *Arch. Gen. Psychiat.*, 1985, 42:937–947.

Gittelman-Klein, R., Spitzer, R., & Cantwell, D.: Diagnostic classifications and psychopharmacological indications. In: J. Werry (Ed.), *Pediatric psychopharmacology: The use of behavior modifying drugs in children*. New York: Brunner/Mazel, 1978.

Goldman, J., Stein, C. L., & Guerry, S.: *Psychological methods of child assessment*. New York: Brunner/Mazel, 1984.

Green, W., Campbell, M., Hardesty, A., Grega, D., Padron-Gayol, M., Shell, J., & Erlenmeyer-Kimling, L.: A comparison of schizophrenic and autistic children. *J. Am. Acad. Child Psychiat.*, 1984, 23:399–409.

Group for the Advancement of Psychiatry (GAP): *Psychopathological disorders in childhood*. New York: Jason Aronson, 1974.

Henderson, S.: The assessment of "clumsy" children: Old and new approaches. *J. Child Psychol. Psychiat.*, 1987, 28:511–527.

Jacob, T., & Tennenbaum, D.: Family assessment methods in child psychopathology. In: M. Rutter, H. Tuma, & I. Lann (Eds.), *Assessment and diagnoses*. New York: Guilford Press, 1988, pp. 196–231.

Kanner, L.: *Child psychiatry*. Springfield, IL: Charles C Thomas, 1935.

Kanner, L.: *Child psychiatry* (3rd ed.). Springfield, IL: Charles C Thomas, 1962, pp. 726–751.

Kashani, J., Orvachel, H., Burk, J., & Reid, J.: Informant variance: The issue of parent-child disagreement. *J. Am. Acad. Child Psychiat.*, 1985, 24:437–441.

Klein, D., Taylor, E., Dickstein, S., & Harding, K.: The early-late onset distinction in DSM-III-R Dysthymia. *J. Affect. Disorders*, 1988, 14:25–33.

Kolvin, I., Berney, T., & Bhate, S.: Classification and diagnosis of Depression in School Phobia. *Br. J. Psychiat.*, 1984, 145:347–357.

Kovacs, M.: A developmental perspective on methods and measures in the assessment of Depressive Disorders: The clinical interview. In: M. Rutter, C. Izard, & P. Read (Eds.), *Depression in young people: Clinical and developmental perspectives*. New York: Guilford Press, 1986.

Kovacs, M., Feinberg, T., Crouse-Novak, M., Paulauskas, S., & Finkelstein, R.: Depressive Disorders in children: I. A longitudinal prospective study of characteristics and recovery. *Arch. Gen. Psychiat.*, 1984a, 41:229–239.

Kovacs, M., Feinberg, T., Crouse-Novak, M., Paulauskas, S., Pollock, M., & Finkelstein, R.: Depressive Disorders in childhood: II. A longitudinal study of the risk for a subsequent Major Depression. *Arch. Gen. Psychiat.*, 1984b, 41:643–649.

Lahey, B., Schaughnecy, E., Strauss, C., & Frame, C.: Are Attention Deficit Disorders With and Without Hyperactivity similar or dissimilar disorders? *J. Am. Acad. Child Psychiat.*, 1984, 23:302–309.

Last, C., Hersen, M., Kazdin, A., et al.: Comparison of DSM-III Separation Anxiety, and Overanxious Disorders: Demographic characteristics and patterns of comorbidity. *J. Am. Acad. Child Adol. Psychiat.*, 1987, 26:527–531.

Leonard, H.: Drug treatment of Obsessive Compulsive Disorder. In: J. Rapoport (Ed.), *Obsessive Compulsive Disorder in children and adolescents*. Washington, D.C.: American Psychiatric Press, Inc., 1989.

Leonard, H., & Rapoport, J.: Anxiety Disorders in childhood and adolescence. In: A. Tasman (Ed.), *American Psychiatric Association Annual Review* (Vol. 8). Washington, D.C.: American Psychiatric Press, Inc., 1989.

Leonard, H., Swedo, S., Rapoport, J., Coltey, M., & Cheslow, D.: Treatment of childhood Obsessive-Compulsive Disorder with clomipramine and desmethylimipramine: A double-blind cross-over comparison. *Psychopharmacol. Bull.*, 1988, 24:93–95.

McKnew, D., Cytryn, L., Buchsbaum, M., Hamovit, J., Lamour, M., Rapoport, J., & Gershon, E.: Lithium response in children of lithium responding parents. *Psychiatr Res.*, 1981, 4:171–180.

Mendlewicz, J., & Baron, M.: Morbidity risks in subtypes of unipolar depressive illness: Differences between early and late onset forms. *Br. J. Psychiat.*, 1981, 139:463–466.

Nee, L., Caine, E., Polinsky, R., Eldridge, R., & Ebert, M.: Gilles de la Tourette syndrome: A clinical and family study of fifty cases. *Ann. Neurol.*, 1980, 1(7):41–49.

O'Leary, K., & Carr, E.: Childhood disorders. In: G. Wilson & C. Franks (Eds.), *Contemporary behavior therapy: Conceptual foundations of clinical practice*. New York: Guilford Press, 1982.

Ornitz, E., & Ritvo, E.: The syndrome of autism: A critical review. *Am. J. Psychiat.*, 1976, 133(6):609–621.

Petty, L. K., Ornitz, E. M., Mistelman, J. D., et al.: Autistic children who became schizophrenic. *Arch. Gen. Psychiat.*, 1984, 41:129–135.

Prendergast, M., Taylor, E., Rapoport, J., Bartko, J., Donnelly, M., Zametkin, A., Ahearn, M. B., Dunn, G., & Wieselberg, H. M.: The diagnosis of childhood Hyperactivity: A U.S.-U.K. cross-national study of DSM-III and ICD-9. *J. Child Psychol. Psychiat.*, 1988, 29:284–300.

Puig-Antich, J.: The use of RDC criteria for Major Depressive Disorder in children and adolescents. *J. Am. Acad. Child Psychiat.*, 1982, 21:291–293.

Puig-Antich, J.: Psychobiological markers: Effects of age and puberty. In: M. Rutter, C. Izard, & P. Read (Eds.), *Depression in young people: Developmental and clinical perspectives*. New York: Guilford Press, 1986.

Rapoport, J.: DSM-III-R and pediatric psychopharmacology. In: J. Rapoport & K. Conners (Eds.), *Special Issue, Psychopharmacol. Bull.*, 1985, 21:803–806.

Rapoport, J.: DSM-III-R and child psychiatry. In: C. Last & M. Hersen (Eds.), *Issues in diagnostic research.* New York: Plenum Press, 1987a.

Rapoport, J.: Pediatric psychopharmacology: The last decade. In: H. Meltzer (Ed.), *Psychopharmacology: The third generation of progress.* New York: Raven Press, 1987b, pp. 1211–1214.

Rapoport, J. (Ed.): *Obsessive Compulsive Disorder in children and adolescents.* Washington D.C.: American Psychiatric Press, Inc., 1989.

Rapoport, J. & Benoit, M.: The relation of direct home observations to the clinic evaluation of hyperactive school age boys. *J. Child Psychol. Psychiat.,* 1975, 16:141–147.

Rapoport, J., & Conners, K. (Eds.): Rating scales and assessment instruments for use in pediatric psychopharmacology research. *Psychopharmacol. Bull.,* 1985, DHHS Publication No. (ADM) 86-173, 21(4):713–1124.

Reich, W., & Earls, F.: Rules for making psychiatric diagnoses in children on the basis of multiple sources of information: Preliminary strategies. *J. Abnorm. Child Psychol.,* 1987, 15:601–616.

Rey, J., Bashir, M., Schwarz, M., Richards, I., Plapp, J., & Stewart, G.: Oppositional Disorder: Fact or fiction? *J. Am. Acad. Child. Adol. Psychiat.,* 1988, 27:157–162.

Rosenthal, N., Carpenter, C., James, S., Pany, B., Rogers, S., & Wehr, T.: Seasonal Affective Disorder in childhood and adolescence. *Am. J. Psychiat.,* 1986, 143:356–358.

Russell, A., Cantwell, D., Mattison, R., & Will, L.: A comparison of DSM-II and DSM-III in the diagnosis of childhood psychiatric disorders: III. Multiaxial features. *Arch. Gen. Psychiat.,* 1979, 36:1223–1226.

Rutter, M.: DSM-III-R: A postscript. In: M. Rutter, A. H. Tuma, & I. Lann (Eds.), *Assessment and diagnosis in child psychopathology.* New York: Guilford Press, 1988.

Rutter, M.: Diagnosis and definition. In: M. Rutter, & E. Schopler (Eds.), *Autism: A reappraisal of concepts and treatment.* New York: Plenum Press, 1978.

Rutter, M., & Graham, P.: The reliability and validity of the psychiatric assessment of the child. I. Interview with the child. *Br. J. Psychiat.,* 1968, 114:563–579.

Rutter, M., Izard, C., & Read, P.: *Depression in young people: Clinical and developmental perspectives.* New York: Guilford Press, 1986.

Rutter, M., Lebovici, S., Eisenberg, L., Snezvenskij, A., Sadoun, R., Brooke, E., & Lin, T.: A triaxial classification of mental disorders in childhood. *J. Child Psychol. Psychiat.,* 1979, 10:41–61.

Rutter, M., & Schopler, E.: *Autism.* New York: Plenum Press, 1978.

Rutter, M., Shaffer, D., & Shepherd, M.: *A multiaxial classification of child psychiatric disorders.* Geneva: World Health Organization, 1975.

Rutter, M., Tizard, J., & Whitmore, K.: *Education, health and behavior: Psychological and medical study of childhood development.* New York: Wiley, 1970.

Rutter, M., Tuma, A., & Lann, I.: *Assessment and diagnosis in child psychopathology.* New York: Guilford Press, 1988.

Shaffer, D., Schonfeld, I., Trautman, P., et al.: Neurological soft signs. *Arch. Gen. Psychiat.,* 1978, 42:342–351.

Shaffer, D., Gould, M. S., Brasic, J., et al.: Children's Global Assessment Scale [CGAS]. *Arch. Gen. Psychiat.,* 1983, 40:1228–1231.

Shapiro, A., Shapiro, E., & Wayne, H.: Treatment of Tourette's syndrome. *Arch. Gen. Psychiat.,* 1973, 28:92–97.

Spitzer, R., & Cantwell, D.: The DSM-III classification of psychiatric disorders of infancy, childhood and adolescence. *J. Am. Acad. Child Psychiat.,* 1980, 19:356–370.

Sprague, R., & Baxley, G.: Drugs for behavior management, with comment on some legal aspects. In J. Wortis (Ed.), Mental retardation and developmental disabilities (Vol. X). New York: Brunner/Mazel, 1978.

Stephens, R., Bartley, L., Rapoport, J., & Berg, C.: A brief preschool playroom interview: Correlates with independent behavioral reports. *J. Am. Acad. Child Psychiat.,* 1980, 19:213–224.

Stewart, M. A., deBlois, C. S., & Cummings, C.: Psychiatric disorder in the parents of hyperactive boys and those with Conduct Disorder. *J. Child Psychol. Psychiat.*, 1980, 21:283–292.

Tanguay, P., & Asarnow, R.: Schizophrenia in children. In: R. Michels & J. Cavenar (Eds.), *Psychiatry.* Philadelphia: Lippincott, 1985.

Tantam, D.: Asperger's syndrome. *J. Child Psychol. Psychiat.*, 1988, 29:245–255.

Taylor, E.: Attention Deficit and Conduct Disorder syndromes. In: M. Rutter, A. Tuma, & I. Lann (Eds.), *Assessment and diagnosis in child psychopathology.* New York: Guilford Press, 1988, pp. 377–408.

van der Kolk, B.: Adolescent vulnerability to Post-traumatic Stress Disorder. *Psychiatry*, 1985, 48:365–370.

van Goor-Lambo, G.: The reliability of Axis V of the multiaxial classification scheme. *J. Child Psychol. Psychiat.*, 1987, 28:597–612.

Wallerstein, J.: Children of divorce: Stress and developmental tasks. In: N. Garnerzy & M. Rutter (Eds.), *Stress, coping and development in children.* New York: McGraw-Hill, 1983, pp. 265–302.

Weiner, J. (Ed.): *Psychopharmacology in childhood and adolescence.* New York: Basic Books, 1977.

Weissman, M., Merikangas, K., Wickramaratne, P., Kidd, K., Prosoff, A., Leckman, J., & Pauls, D.: Understanding the clinical heterogeneity of Major Depression using family data. *Arch. Gen. Psychiat.*, 1986, 43:430–434.

Welner, A., Welner, Z., & Fishman, R.: Psychiatric adolescent inpatients: Eight to ten year follow-up. *Arch. Gen. Psychiat.*, 1979, 36:698–700.

Welner, Z., Reich, W., Herjanic, B., Jung, K. G., Amado, H.: Reliability, validity and parent-child agreement: Studies of the Diagnostic Interview for Children and Adolescents (DICA). *J. Am. Acad. Child. Adol. Psychiat.*, 1987, 26:649–653.

Werry, J. (Ed.): *Pediatric psychopharmacology: The use of behavior modifying drugs in children.* New York: Brunner/Mazel, 1978.

Wing, L. & Gould, J.: Severe impairments of social interaction and associated abnormalities in children: Epidemiology and classification. *J. Autism Dev. Disorders*, 1979, 9:11–30.

Wolff, S.: Symptomatology and outcome of preschool children with Behavior Disorders attending a child guidance clinic. *J. Child Psychol. Psychiat.*, 1961, 2:269–276.

Wolff, S. & Chick, J.: Schizoid Personality in childhood: A controlled followup study. *Psychol. Med.*, 1980, 10:85–100.

Index